WEISER ♀ CLASSICS

THE WEISER CLASSICS SERIES represents the full range of subjects and genres that have been part of Weiser's publishing program for over sixty years, from tarot, divination, and magick to alchemy and esoteric philosophy. Drawing on Weiser's extensive backlist, the series offers works by renowned authors and spiritual teachers, foundational texts, as well as introductory guides on an array of topics.

———————

FUTHARK

FUTHARK

A HANDBOOK OF
RUNE MAGIC

REVISED EDITION

EDRED THORSSON

**WEISER
BOOKS**

This edition first published in 2020 by Weiser Books, an imprint of
Red Wheel/Weiser, LLC
With offices at:
65 Parker Street, Suite 7
Newburyport, MA 01950
www.redwheelweiser.com

ISBN: 978-1-57863-700-3
Library of Congress Cataloging-in-Publication Data available upon request.

Series Editors
Mike Conlon, Production Director, Red Wheel/Weiser Books
Judika Illes, Editor-at-Large, Weiser Books
Peter Turner, Associate Publisher, Weiser Books

Series Design
Kathryn Sky-Peck, Creative Director, Red Wheel/Weiser

Interior images by Edred Thorsson
Typeset in Palatino

Printed in Canada
MAR
10 9 8 7 6 5 4

OÐNI

Contents

Foreword

I FIRST BECAME AWARE of the runes back in the 60s or early 70s through a TV dramatization of M. R. James's short story *Casting the Runes*, in which a wicked antiquarian scholar uses them to put a fatal curse on his enemies. For a long time after that rather jaundiced introduction I would have been hard pressed to give an intelligent account of what the runes really were. In my mind, they were little more than primitive signs, crudely hewn in stone or wood long ago by barbarian hands. And in truth this is what they would have meant at that time to the average person—if they meant anything at all. Literature in English on the subject was scarce apart from some highly academic works by runologists and scholars of Old Norse. Around the 1980s, that situation began to change as a wider reading public was introduced to the runes. The present work, which first appeared in 1984, played a key role in this regard. Other works that contributed to the runic revival included Ralph Blum's divinatory *Rune Book* (1982) and Freya Aswynn's *Leaves of Yggdrasil* (1988).

As I became better informed about the runes, I came to realize what a remarkable system they are. In appearance, like the letters of the Celtic Ogham alphabet, with which they have certain things in common, they possess a stark, laconic simplicity. But that very simplicity is an indication of their immense sophistication. By referring to familiar things—such as cattle, torch, hail, gift, ice, birch, lake—they point to primal essences. They take us, via the mundane and specific, into the universal. Take for example the first letter of the runic alphabet, *Fehu*. The name Fehu in Old Norse means "cattle," which to the Nordic peoples was another way of saying wealth, one of the possible meanings of the letter when the runes are used for divination. On a more primal level, as Edred Thorsson tells us, this rune is "the raw archetypal energy of motion and expansion in the universe." In shape, Fehu is traditionally made up of three strokes—one vertical and two right-leaning—whereas other runes are made up of anything between one and five strokes. The strokes turn out to have their own significance, as the Norwegian researcher Halvard Hårklau has shown.[1] By a complex process, involving counting strokes and arranging the runes into groups and columns, he discovered unexpected numerical symmetries, Pythagorean proportions and—most striking of all—a correspondence with the trigrams of the Chinese *Ba-Gua* divination system.

The degree of sophistication that must have gone into the creation of the runes, together with the fact that they evidently appeared rather suddenly about two thousand years ago, would seem to indicate that they were created systematically by some individual, or more likely a group of elders, bards, or sages, and then passed on from tribe to tribe. Here we may possibly learn something from the history of the Ogham alphabet, which is said to have been invented by an Irish bard called Ogma. If something similar happened in the case of the runes, this would explain how they spread very rapidly, and in a relatively consistent form, over a large swath of northern Europe. The original runic alphabet has 24 letters and is known as the Elder Futhark. Some seven centuries later a reduced alphabet with 16 letters was created, known as the Younger Futhark—the name Futhark being derived from the first six letters.

Like Odin, who discovered their secrets, the runes are manifold, and their uses go far beyond divination. There exist various systems of what one might call runic yoga, in which each rune has a corresponding body position. The runes can also be used as mantras, as objects of meditation, as talismans and as capsules of energy in magical work. In dealing with each rune, Edred Thorsson gives its corresponding key words, sounds, body posture, and qualities for use in magical workings. He is eminently well qualified to write about the subject, as he is both a runemaster and a scholar who is well versed in the Germanic languages including Old Norse and has a deep knowledge of the corresponding lore and literature.

The main part of the book, dealing with the individual runes, is preceded by a valuable survey of their origin, history and lore, mentioning some of the avatars of the runic revival such as the Austrian mystical writer and folklorist Guido von List who, in the early twentieth century, posited a runic alphabet of 18 letters instead of the 24 of the Elder Futhark or the 16 of the Younger—it is perhaps a measure of the vitality of the runes that successive runologists have continued to produce

---

1 See my book *Beyond the North Wind* (Newburyport, MA: Weiser Books, 2019), pp 72-74.

different theories about the origin of the letters and their authentic order. Later chapters deal with the use of the runes in magic, and there are valuable appendices that include a guide to Old Norse pronunciation and a table of runic correspondences.

Futhark has justifiably established itself as a classic among works on the runes over the nearly four decades since its original publication, and this new and improved edition of the book is to be warmly welcomed. In the age of the Internet and the global village, the runes now speak to people of all regions. As the author writes in his eloquent poem at the end of the book, the runes still "bloom forth, roaring their songs."

—Christopher McIntosh
author of *Beyond the North Wind*

List of Abbreviations

All translations from Old Norse, Old English, and other old languages found in this book are those of the author. An attempt has been made to strike a balance between poetic and literal translation, but often favor is given to the literal for the sake of correct understanding. In such cases, notes may be added.

A-S	Anglo-Saxon (OE)
GMC	Germanic
GO	Gothic
MS	Manuscript
OE	Old English
ON	Old Norse
pl.	plural
sig.	singular

Transcriptions of Old Norse Terms

Certain special Germanic graphics have been transliterated in this book. The following are in keeping with certain spelling conventions of the Middle Ages:

ð	dh
þ	th
ǫ	ö

Preface to the 2020 Edition

A BOOK HAS A LIFE, it has its own destiny (*ørlög*) and word-glory. *Futhark*, as a book, is akin to a battle-scarred warrior of old who is still among us to recount the ways of earlier days. There is nothing more authentic to the essence of knowledge infused with the enthusiasm of youth than to read the words of the young pioneer. This new edition of our old friend, *Futhark: A Handbook of Rune Magic*, comes over forty years after the text was completed in 1979.

I first began to pursue the task of seeking the mysteries of the runes after I audibly "heard" the sound "RUNA" on a summer day in 1974. I was just twenty-one years old. My research and inner work led me to complete a hand-written manuscript on rune magic in 1975. This was an immature work that came to be called "A Primer of Runic Magic." I tried to get it published. A major mainstream house expressed interest and promised a contract. But ultimately the editor wrote and informed me that the marketing department said that "runes wouldn't sell." You can imagine my disappointment. But I took it as a sign from my other-worldly mentor, Woden, that I should keep working and revise the work in light of the great new things I was learning in the academic setting. By 1979 I had completed the text of *Futhark* as it eventually appeared in 1984. But the challenges for this book were not yet over. A respected publisher gave me a contract for the book— but for various reasons was not in a position to bring the book out. Underlying it all was probably the same idea that "runes" were just not a category people knew any-thing about. By 1981, it was clear that the book would not be published. The contract was returned to me and I called Donald Weiser. *Futhark* finally had found a house with the courage, ability, and vision to release it to the world.

Futhark had a fresh, youthful edge to it. Yet, at the same time, it was informed by the best academic sources. Attention has been given in the new edition to retain everything of the original energy, and to correct any errors of fact and expand information on certain points. This new edition should be considered a state-of-the-art *Futhark*.

After the publication of *Futhark* I subsequently wrote necessary expansions on my esoteric runic researches, which included *Runelore* (Weiser, 1987), *Runecaster's Handbook* (Weiser, 1988), and more recently *Alu* (Weiser, 2012). Another significant continuation of the foundation laid in *Futhark* remains the systematic runic curriculum found in *The Nine Doors of Midgard*, first published in 1991. In many ways everything I have written (now over fifty books) has been the result of that one word, RUNA, I heard in the summer of 1974— and before that the observation of an occultation of Venus on March 11, 1959 in Denison, Texas when I was five years old.

Two significant alterations to the content of the original edition of *Futhark* include more precise information on the transliteration of modern English into runes and a revision of Tarot correspondences in Appendix D based on the results of my research published in *The Magian Tarok* (Inner Traditions, 2019).

The book *Futhark* remains a magical text on many levels. It constituted the first reliable, authentic, in-depth introduction of esoteric runology for the twentieth century. This is the meaning behind its title: f.u.th.a.r.k as a representation of the beginning of an orderly study. Also, perhaps largely unnoticed on a conscious level by most readers of the original edition is the poem that concluded the main body of the text. I have included commentary on the original purpose and meaning of that poem in this new edition.

For older students of *Futhark*, as well as for those reading the book for the first time, it is my greatest wish that this text can open your eyes to a sense of the hidden, which will motivate you to seek the mysteries and wax in wisdom and well-being.

Preface to 1984 Edition

THE PRESENT WORK IS ACTUALLY a second version of a manuscript originally written in the *Armanen*-system, which was completed in 1976. Soon thereafter, I discovered the deeper, long hidden power of the Elder Runic Tradition—which is transpersonal and fundamentally independent of the misinterpretations and manipulations of uninformed individuals. This misinformation has unfortunately been the hallmark of almost all books on operant runelogy that have appeared in recent years. In 1979, the revised manuscript of *Futhark* was complete. However, it has taken four years for it to find a publisher with the ability to bring it before a readership. During the intervening years, I have continued my investigations into the runes on all levels, and some of my ideas have evolved—based upon exoteric as well as esoteric work. Almost no changes have been made in the 1979 version, however, since it was and is fundamentally sound due to its foundation in the eternal *traditional* futhark-system. It is hoped that these more developed ideas will also be able to find a larger audience, and it is to that end that the Institute for Runic Studies, Ásatrú, and the Rune-Gild were founded in 1980. As it stands, *Futhark* remains the first step in learning the "ABC's" of the esoteric wisdom of our Germanic heritage.

Introduction

MUCH HAS BEEN WRITTEN about the runes and their magical power over the past several decades. However, this book was the first in the English language to delve into the practical magical uses of the ancient Germanic runes and the system they embody, and in which they are in turn contained. It was the avowed intention of this work to rectify the great lack of practical material on the runes in English, to deal with the operative side of the half-forgotten, much neglected runic system of magic and mysticism. This is still one of the most powerful forms of metaphysical thought available to the Westerner and one that he developed.

The roots of runic tradition have been hidden from our view for several hundred years, but now the long-awaited age has arrived, in which the power of the runic mysteries will again become manifest. Among English-speaking magicians, rune knowledge had been steadily on the decline since the days of King Cnute (died c. 1035), but their lore never completely died out—especially in Scandinavia, where runic incantations (*galdrar*) continued to be practiced until fairly recent times.

This work is intended to invoke the runic force in the minds of all men and women, so that their lore and mysterious power may again be born to rise to the level of their former splendor in the English-speaking world. The runes embody the greatest and the smallest secrets of nature, and they are the keys to those secrets—for they are indeed the secrets themselves. Too long have these magnificent tools of magic been allowed to atrophy in dusty tomes. Now their ways are again made known to those who would be wise.

Rune lore represents an important part of the oldest tradition of initiatory wisdom-magic known to the Germanic world. The ancient Goths, Scandinavians, Germans, and English all knew the power of the runes, and they were bound together by a mighty guild of runemasters, who taught their craft throughout all the tribes of Northern Europe. It would seem wise for the descendants of these forebears to turn to the runic power to regain the depths of their hoary wisdom. For if we are to believe their lore, these ancestors never died but rather were reborn, generation after generation, always keeping their secrets with them—until now, *they* are *us*. Through the runic keys *we* may again unlock these secret recesses of the soul and thus unleash wisdom and magical power for our own use today.

The runes and the runic system, as an eternal expression of world laws, may be constantly put to new uses without in any way violating their timeless and archaic characteristics. Therefore, they are now used in systems of psychological integration and cosmological investigation—both of which are actually firmly based on precepts found in the Eddas.

One of the most potent aspects of the runic system of magic and philosophy is its openness and lack of dogmatism. Information given in this book is intended to be a guide for the talented and inventive *vitki* (magician), who should use it as a stepping stone toward becoming a true philosopher in his or her own right. Again, the traditions of the Eddas and sagas are the best indicators of the spiritual directions the vitki should take in order to get the best results. In ancient times every free man was his own priest—so it should be today. As far as a plan of development and initiation is concerned, it is suggested that the aspiring vitki should read through the entire book, developing a personal version from the complete system given in the following pages. However, today there does exist a Rune-Gild that provides a more systematic initiation for the dedicated *vitkar*. Its curriculum can be found in *The Nine Doors of Midgard* (The Rune-Gild, 2016). The present book is divided into three main sections, containing the knowledge, theory, and practice of runecraft. This, coupled with other viable books on magic, forms the basis for a fairly advanced level of initiation. It is impossible to express the vastness of a system as all-encompassing as the Kabbalah or Vedic literature in a book of this or any other length. Putting even this basic system of mainly practical rune magic in one volume has been quite difficult. It is hoped that further interest in the runes will be kindled, so that future books dealing with divination, cosmology, wisdom-lore, and so forth, may be produced.

There have been several books and articles written in the last few years that connected the National Socialist movement in Germany with the runic cult and rune magic. Indeed, the Nazis made use of the runic forms in their most external aspects, akin to what we might call "branding" today. The beginning rune vitki of today may take some strange comfort from the fact that the runes did continue to show themselves to be such potent symbols in the twentieth century! But it must be strongly emphasized that the runes and indeed the Germanic spirit itself was *not* at the heart of this "bureaucratic blasphemy," but rather it was a sort of pseudo-Christian messianic Manicheanism that owned the soul of the Nazi Party. Much of the historical background of the runic aspects of the Nazi movement will be discussed in the first chapter of this book, for only through a thorough understanding of its misdirection of our most sacred treasures may we truly put its unwelcome specter to rest once and for all!

An endeavor has been made throughout this book to remain as close as possible to the traditional *form* and *spirit* of rune lore and to present a system as free as possible from any Judeo-Christian influence. Too long has the Westerner suffered "bearing the cross of alien fruits." They have had their chance and have failed time and again in their impotent effort to satisfy the depths of the IndoEuropean soul. Their aeon has come to an end; the time is ripe for a reemergence of the wisdom of the *Eriloz* (the vitki). The breakthrough of holy power must take place within the soul of each individual—and it is in this hope that this work has been wrought.

For information on the Rune-Gild, of which the author was the founder, readers are invited to make contact at: *www.rune-gild.org*

CHAPTER 1

RUNE KNOWLEDGE

Definitions

The first step in understanding rune lore is the understanding of the concept *rune*. A rune is not merely a letter in an old Germanic alphabet, but rather it bears the primary definition of "secret" or "mysterium." This basic meaning may be easily compared to the use of the term arcana in connection with the Tarot. Therefore, a rune is primarily a secret, holy concept or idea that must be expressed or dealt within concealment. Throughout this work "rune" should be understood first in the sense of a secret and holy concept.

The word *rune* is indigenous to the Germanic group of languages, and it is found in all the ancient Germanic dialects. (See Table 1.1 on page 2.)

The modern German cognate is *raunen*, to whisper. *Rún* is also found in old Celtic languages, where it appears in Old Irish as *rún*. and in Middle Welsh as *rhin*, both with the meaning of mysterium, secret. It is probable that the Celts borrowed the semantic quality of this word from the Germanic languages. *Rune* developed from the Proto-Indo-European root **reu-*, "to roar."

Later this meaning was applied to each hieroglyphic figure that represented a rune—a unit of secret lore. It is this form that is inscribed as a symbol for a formless and timeless idea. Still later this symbol was incorporated into a system of writing that imparted a phonetic value to each symbol form. Now the rune has become mistakenly synonymous with the concept "letter" as expressed in other languages.

Table 1.1. Germanic Rune Definition

Dialect	Word	Meaning
Old Norse	*rún*	secret, secret lore, wisdom; magical signs; written characters.
Gothic	*rúna*	secret, mysterium. Wulfilas, in his fourth-century Gothic translation of the Bible, uses this term to translate the Greek μνστήριον
Old English	*rún*	mystery, secret council.
Old Saxon	*rúna*	mystery, secret
Old High German	*rúna*	mystery, secret

Only a certain number of the various forms of the rune hoard were ever used as phonetic representations (which we will call letter runes), while a large number remained more or less within the purely ideographic realm. This latter group may be referred to as glyph runes. This work primarily deals with the letter runes and the magical system in which they developed, although the glyph runes are an integral part of this system as well. It must be kept in mind that both groups are equally runic. The letter runes were "standardized" in the futhark system by the magical guilds of the time, according to particular numerological and conceptual criteria.

Magical Definitions

According to most scholars, the runes were ancient symbols used in writing, mainly on stone or metal. These symbols bore religious or magical significance for the people who inscribed them—this cannot be denied by the most dreary of scholars.

For the rune vitki, however, the signs take on a much richer and more expanded meaning that reveals their true nature and power as well as their historical and cosmic significance. The vitki sees hieroglyphs of a highly complex nature in the forms of the runes. Investigation and research into intellectual and magical realms have revealed the runes as ideographs expressing a process and flow of force and energy.

Each rune has a threefold nature, which is also the threefold essence of the secret slumbering within it. The points are:

Form (ideograph and phonetic value)

Idea (symbolic content)

Number (its dynamic nature, revealing its relationship to other runes).

Runes describe energy flows and states as related to the self, to the planet, and ultimately to the multiverse. The runes summarize and graphically express separate world concepts that can be used as focal points for magical and mystical operations, both singly and in combination.

The Origin of the Runes

Here we speak more of the origin of the runic shapes than of the origins of the mysteries they represent. The actual mysteries are timeless and were created—or more properly "came into being"—with the emergence of the Nine Worlds out of *Ginnungagap* (the magically charged void). In fact, the runes are important agents in this process of "creation" or "shaping" and precede the arising of animate beings in the Worlds. The runic forms may be spoken of in a somewhat more historical context. These shapes are ultimately born from the holy signs conceived in the minds of the Bronze Age priests and magicians (and probably much earlier) as abstract graphic expressions of the innermost content of their religious and magical teachings. (See Figure 1.1) They are found in great abundance on the most ancient rock carvings of Scandinavia. Rudolf John Gorsleben describes the "primal man" sitting atop a mountain receiving conceptual flashes of inspiration, which he then emotionally expresses in markings that come to *be* those concepts.

Figure 1.1. Some Bronze Age ideographic rock-carving configurations that were to evolve into runic shapes.

In the earliest period these so-called "pre-runic" signs remained totally ideographic, or hieroglyphic. However, when contact was made with the Mediterranean cultures, the notion of phonetically representing language by symbols was slowly introduced into the Germanic territories. Many scholars believe that this introduction began in the second century BCE, when the Cimbri and Teutones invaded the Italian peninsula and came into contact with the North Etruscan and Latin alphabets; while others believe that the runes were ultimately formulated by the Goths in the first and second centuries CE, while that tribe was still on the Baltic coast. These theories are all very interesting and hold many truths, but this is not our main interest. It is important to notice that when the Germanic peoples chose a rune (cultic sign) to represent a sound in their language, they would usually (but not always) choose a shape that in some way resembled the corresponding Etruscan, Latin, or Greek character. This undoubtedly plays a large role in the formulation of galdrar (number formulas) and their associations with certain runic forms.

The internal structure, ordering, naming, and symbolic content of these glyphs are totally unaffected by the Mediterranean cultures. There is a magical deep-structure that governs these factors. This deep-structure was well known by the priests and magicians of the Germanic cult, and they carefully formulated the runic ideology and transmitted it across tribal boundaries through preexisting cultic channels. Through this ancient guild of runemasters the runic system was able to maintain a high level of internal integrity despite crossing countless tribal lines over several centuries. As early as the first century CE, Tacitus describes the runes (which he calls *notae* in Latin) being used in fully developed divinatory rites.

Mythically, it is through the "God of Magic," Ódhinn, that the gods and men are able to receive rune wisdom. Ódhinn is the first being to be fully initiated into the runic mysteries; that is, he first extracted the rune wisdom directly from its source and formulated it within his being in such a way that it could be *communicated* to other beings. Therefore, it is through the Ódhinic force that the runes may be perceived best. This initiatory myth is represented in the *Elder*, or *Poetic Edda*, in the song called "Hávamál," "the sayings of Hár" (Hár: the High One, Ódhinn). Stanzas 138 and 139 of this song read:

I know, that I hung
on the windy tree
all of the nights nine,
wounded by spear
and given to Ódhinn;
myself to myself,
on that tree,
which no man knows,
from what roots it rises.
They dealt me no bread
nor drinking horn,
I looked down,
I took up the runes
I took them screaming,
I fell back from there.

This describes an initiatory process, which seems to some similar to a shamanistic type, in which the initiate passes through the Nine Worlds of the World-Tree to the realm of *Hel* (Death) and momentarily enters her sphere. At that moment the initiate receives the entire body of rune wisdom, and it is etched into his being. In the next instant, the initiate returns to Midhgardhr with the rune wisdom permanently encoded and ready for use and communication.

History of the Runes

The runic system was perhaps fully developed by as early as 200 BCE. It is certain that the magico-religious practices of the ancient Germanic priesthood were aided by the use of many runic and or pre-runic signs for we still see these etched into stone all over Scandinavia.

The ideographic stage of runic development is the cradle of rune magic. In this earliest period the ideographs would appear in isolation. Soon, however, magical sound and number formulas (*galdrar*) began to be produced, which were intended to have particular magical effects. Not long after this development the runes were being used to write in the common Germanic dialect. In all of these stages of development magical considerations were primary. All three types of runic formulations—ideographic, sound-formulaic, and phonetic word representations—continued to be used side by side, and thus all three modes are valid for our modern runic practices. Examples of these types will be provided and interpreted in the practical sections of the book. Runes have been found carved on wood, stone, metal, and bone objects. Unfortunately, the vast majority of the runic talismans were crafted in wood—which of course rotted rather quickly. It is most important to remember that the runes were born from a magical tradition, not a purely linguistic one, and that this magical association never left them.

As mentioned above, the runes began to be used to represent language phonetically soon after the Germanic peoples came into contact with the Mediterranean cultures in the second century BCE. It was then also that they were standardized into a set row of runic signs, which we come to call the Elder Futhark. Inscriptions remain the principal mode of crafting runes. The greatest number of runic inscriptions are on runestones, of which approximately twenty-five hundred are known (there is a total of almost five thousand runic artifacts in all). The runestones were raised as sacred landmarks and memorials all over Scandinavian countries. There are even controversial runestones found in the United States. Runes have marked the path of Nordic trade routes from Eastern Europe to Greenland and from the Arctic Circle to Greece and Constantinople.

Writing and Art

Only a few scattered instances of runes occur in written manuscripts and few of them seem to have any overt magical intent, although they may be reflections of magical practices. Rune poems found in Anglo-Saxon and Scandinavian traditions are of extreme importance, and portions of these will be discussed under certain runes. The oldest manuscript containing runic symbols is the *Abecedarium Nordmannicum* from the ninth century CE. *The Codex Runicus* is a fourteenth-century Danish manuscript written entirely in runes; it contains the laws of the province of Sconia. In the Swedish period of the Thirty Years War (1630-1635), the

Swedish forces of Gustavus Adolphus used the runes as a kind of code to confuse Austrian intelligence.

The glyph runes often are found incorporated into runic inscriptions. The most common of these is the *Thórshamarr* (the hammer of Thórr) or *fylfot* ⌐⌐. This symbol represents the dynamic magical force of the *Æsir* and the explosive power of the Thunderer. The cross, or sun wheel ⊕, also is common from the Bronze Age onward. This ancient common European symbol was used to denote holy places and was later adopted by the Christians in their efforts to convert the folk who used it. More recently, of course, the Nazis revived the runes as manipulative tools and made the *Hakenkreuz* (hook-cross) their symbol, and the Schutzstaffel adopted a double S-rune, ϟϟ as their identifying mark. These latter are to a large degree seen as imbalanced misdirections of the runic forces. For example, the S-rune is a rune of the sun, not of "victory" as such.

As we look around today, we still may see runic forms in proliferation. The peace symbol, so prevalent in the sixties, is in the form of the Ýr-rune of the Younger Futhark (an alternate form of the *eihwaz* and *elhaz* of the elder row). This became a symbol of "death" in the early twentieth century German runology and was used as such by anti-Nazi activists during the war. Ambulances now carry a bright blue Hagall rune (in its later letter-rune form), which even includes a caduceus symbol (see *Hagalaz*, p. 39). These and other examples give rise to the thought that there is surely something emotionally innate in these runic forms that rises to the surface repeatedly—no matter how much some attempt to suppress them with barren "reason."

The art of old Germanic architecture is said by some to preserve runic shapes in the forms of the *Fachwerk* (half-timbered) building style, which has spread all over the world (see Figure 1.2). Originally, the timbers of the Fachwerk were placed in such a way as to form the shape of a rune. The magical significance of this is that the runic power would then be imparted to the building and its inhabitants. This custom continued on into the days when the builders no longer knew why the timbers were laid in these particular ways—it became simple tradition. The now familiar "Dutch hex signs" also are ultimately derived from a runic source.

In the plastic arts we find the famous example of the golden ritual drinking horns of Gallehus. On these horns there are human figures in particular stances and postures that are certainly representations of cultic signs and runes. The style of these figures is employed in this book to represent the various *ránastödhur* (sometimes called "runic *asanas*"). Another, more obscure example of this practice is the so-called Herrgott

Figure 1.2. Examples of runic patterns found in German half-timbered buildings.

von Bentheim (Lord God of Bentheim). This curious piece of statuary is based on a wooden original that was brought into the town of Bentheim from a nearby Thing-stead. The arms of the figure are bent in the shape of the Anglo-Frisian rune ⅄ (see the T-rune on page 58 for an explanation of the symbol complex involved here), The stone reconstruction was then given a Christian significance; however, even today it is used as an object on which solemn oaths are sworn.

Historically, there have been three ancient codifications of the letter runes: The Elder Futhark (24 runes), the Anglo-Saxon or Frisian row (up to 33 runes), and the Norse (or Younger) Futhark (16 runes). (See Figures 1.3, 1.4, and 1.5.) The latter two are modifications of the first one. That these modifications took place within a traditionally controlled cult of some type is well indicated by the methodical manner in which the order and correspondences of the runes were maintained. Information on some of these correspondences may be found in the Table of Correspondences, Appendix D. This book deals more or less exclusively with the system of the Elder Futhark, which was the rule between c. 200 BCE and 800 CE. However, *the other two systems are also magically valid.* The Younger Futhark began to be developed in the seventh century CE, and this development was complete by about 800 CE, while the Anglo-Saxon Futhork was able to survive the Christianization process until the tenth century CE. Among all the various systems, the shapes of individual runes and in many cases their names often would be altered. This sometimes offers us valuable clues and correspondences to their inner nature. Much of this lore will be revealed in the sections on the individual runes.

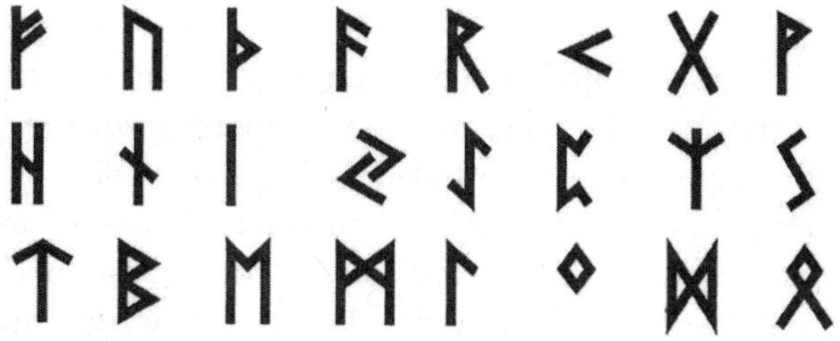

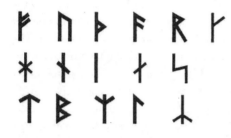

ᚠ ᚢ ᚦ ᚨ ᚱ ᚲ ᚷ ᚹ
ᚺ ᚾ ᛁ ᛃ ᛇ ᛈ ᛉ ᛊ
ᛏ ᛒ ᛖ ᛗ ᛚ ᛜ ᛞ ᛟ

Figure 1.3. The Elder Futhark.

ᚠ ᚢ ᚦ ᚨ ᚱ ᚴ
ᚼ ᚾ ᛁ ᛅ ᛦ
ᛏ ᛒ ᛘ ᛚ ᛯ

Figure 1.4. The Younger Futhark.

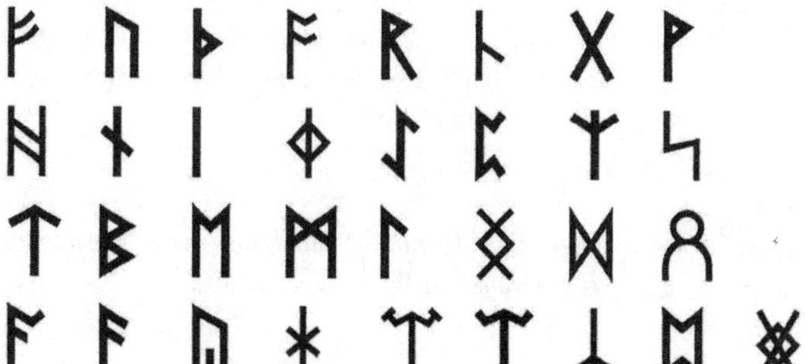

ᚠ ᚢ ᚦ ᚩ ᚱ ᚳ ᚷ ᚹ
ᚻ ᚾ ᛁ ᛄ ᛡ ᛣ ᛠ ᛋ
ᛏ ᛒ ᛖ ᛗ ᛚ ᛝ ᛞ ᛟ
ᚪ ᚫ ᛦ ᚸ ᚣ ᛏ ᛠ ᛢ ᛥ

Figure 1.5. The Anglo-Saxon Futhork.

It is hoped that talented *vitkar* will be inspired by these other systems and develop them further for modern magical practice.

House Marks and Heraldry

In the Middle Ages and after, in the continental Germanic territory, the runes were driven underground, where they found further expression through various graphic arts attributed to the early nobility and farmers. House marks are symbolic or literal monograms, formed from two or more runes often stylistically modified. These house marks were used as identification for property, and in the Middle Ages they were inscribed into objects owned by lord and freeman. In contrast to crests and coats-of-arms, the house mark could be drawn without color and by an unpracticed hand. Although the tradition and form of the house mark grew out of the more elaborate heraldic art, it developed separately from it but was later reincorporated beside the crest. The house mark also could be used as a signature after the fashion of a monogram.

According to Guido von List, the history of house marks is a three-stage development. In the first period, which lasted through the middle of the fifteenth century, the marks still were formed and interpreted according to ancient runes and holy signs, and their value was highly symbolic and cultic. (An example of this is shown in Figure 1.6.)

Figure 1.6. Ideographic German house mark. The symbolic interpretation of this mark has the two thorns of life ᛈ and death ᛦ with the Hammer of Thórr between them. The esoteric reading is "Between life and death may my estate increase and prosper."

Figure 1.7. Runic German house mark. The name FRYDEL is portrayed in this composite form.

Figure 1.8. Monographic German house mark: Latin script forming the initials of a person's name.

The second historical period spans the time from the middle of the fifteenth century to the middle of the eighteenth century. In this era the runic forms of the letters making up the last name, or initials of the first and last names, were welded together into one form (see Figure 1.7.). Here it can be seen that runes have lost their deeper symbolic value in this period. They have been transformed from purely cultic forms to phonetic symbols used to write the name.

After the second historical period (fifteenth to eighteenth century) the use of runes was dropped. Latin script was used, usually to form the initials of a person's name, as shown in Figure 1.8.

Stonemasons' signs, merchants' signs, and masters' signs may in some cases be interpreted according to the same rules that govern the formation and reading of house marks. The three-stage history of house marks is most revealing as to the degeneration of the use of runes into modern times, but by retracing the path the rune vitki may regain some of what otherwise would have been lost.

Heraldic art is an extremely vast topic, and it is beyond the scope of this book to deal with its runic implications. Let it simply and tentatively be said that the runes *may* be found in heraldic art in two ways: (1) they may be embodied in the color pattern that composes the coat-of-arms; or (2) the concept of the rune may be concealed by a symbolic form or figure other than the shape of the runic symbol itself.

A Note on the Tarot and Runes

Some German investigators of this century have guessed that the runes actually are the origin of the Tarot system of the Major Arcana. This may or may not be true—or there may have been some point at which the two systems came into contact. In any event the runes, of course, have a documented past that goes back much farther than documentation for the Tarot. Appendix D offers a system of Tarot correspondences based on the work of the early twentieth century Swedish scholar Sigurd Agrell, and the commentaries on the individual runes occasionally give some interesting parallels. Each interested vitki is invited to come to his or her own conclusions on this matter. (See my *The Magian Tarok* for more information.)

Runic Practices

As mentioned above, the runes are found carved on wood, stone, metal, and bone objects. Wood is most certainly the favorite medium for portraying runes—especially for magical purposes. Words for "pieces of wood" associated with the runes are numerous. Three Old Norse examples of this connection would be the words *stafr* (stave, letter, secret lore), *teinn* (twig, talismanic word for divination), and *hlutr* (lot for divination, talismanic object—on which runes also were carved). There are also a few stone talismans, but of course the large runestones for cultic or funeral-ceremony purposes represent the most numerous runic inscriptions in stone. Metal was extremely popular for talismanic purposes. The *bracteates* (thin metal disks inscribed with runes and various other designs) represent an important tradition in magical runic practice. Other, more utilitarian objects made of metal (especially swords) also were inscribed with runes in order to impart special magical powers to them so that they might perform their function with more distinction—or protect the user. Bone objects also are not uncommon, and these usually are connected with magical practices as well. The runes were carved with either knife points or special pointed instruments dedicated to the *runic* art.

One of the most interesting runic practices is that of further concealing the magical formula with intricately devised codes. These codes were created in order to make the messages more secret—and therefore more effective magically—and also less likely to be understood by the uninitiated. The basis of all the runic codes is the numerical value of the runes. The section of this book dealing with talismanic magic will delve into these traditions on a practical basis.

Both the Younger and Elder Futharks are divided into three groups called *ættir* (families). The futharks represented in Figures 1.3-1.5 are divided in just this way. Through this system a rune may be represented by a twofold numerical formula. For example, : ᚼ : would be indicated by the formula 1:2, because it is the first *aett* and the second rune from the left. This is the basic principle upon which magical runic codes work. It should be noted that in the case of the Younger Futhark a curious and uniform alteration in the order of the ættir took place for purposes of magical codes. (See Figure 1.9).

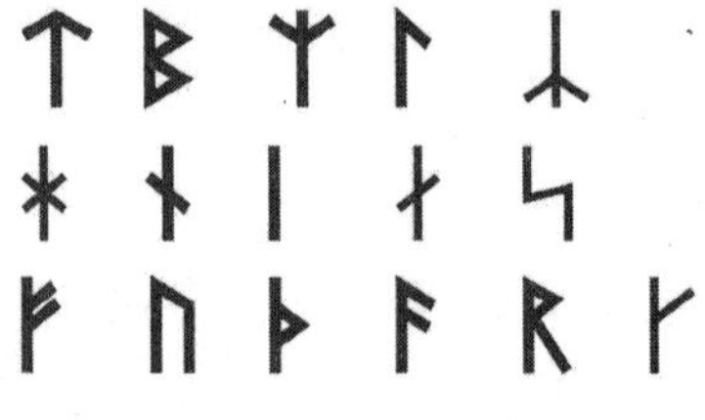

ᛏ ᛒ ᛦ ᛁ ᛅ

ᚼ ᛆ ᛁ ᛂ ᛑ

ᚠ ᚢ ᚦ ᚨ ᚱ ᚴ

Figure 1.9. Coded runic order, altered from the "normal" order of the Younger Futhark (Figure 1.4).

These cryptic runic systems were most highly developed in the Younger Futhark period; however, they most certainly were known and used in the older period, since ancient representations of the elder row are also clearly divided into ættir. Two of the most remarkable methods of making secret runic codes are known by the names branch runes (ON *kvistrúnar*) and tent runes (ON *tjaldrúnar*). An example of the tent-rune method is shown in Figure 1.10.

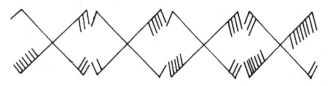

Figure 1.10. Tent-rune method, used here to spell the name thorvaldr.

These tjaldrúnar should be read in a clockwise direction, beginning on the left. Hence, a numerical formula of 1:3, 3:7, 1:5, 1:2, 1:4, 3:5, 3:8, 2:7 appears. (First ætt third rune reads Þ, "th," etc.) The kvistrúnar work in a similar way, except one may portray a single rune with a single glyph in this system. An example representing the magical formula *ek vitki* (I, the Magician) appears in Figure 1.11. The strokes to the left of the vertical indicate the row and those to the right reveal the runic position. Note that a change of word in the formula is indicated by the upward or downward direction of the ætt stroke. The ninth-century St. Gall MS 270 portrays several more cryptographic systems of rune writing.

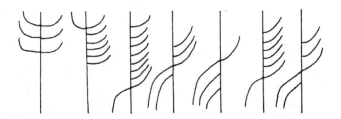

Figure 1.11. Branch runes representing the magical formula ek vitki (I the Magician).

Runes may be magically used in a wide variety of ways. The most common method of rune magic in days of yore was probably talismanic— that is, runes were inscribed into various objects and infused with psychic power in order to effect some change in the vitki or his environment. A dramatic example of this is provided by the *Egilssaga,* chapter 44, where we read that the hero, Egill, suspects that there is poison in a drink that has been given to him, so he stabs the palm of his hand, carves runes on the drinking horn, and colors the runic forms with the blood. The horn shatters and the poison flows away. Hundreds of runic talismans have survived. Today we may study these in order to gain a deeper under-standing of the magical techniques used to create them. The use of poetic *runagaldrar* (runic incantations) also was quite common as a method. The *Poetic Edda*, as well as numerous runic artifacts, speak with the voice of many of these ancient runic incantations. The practice of *stadhagaldr* (pos-ture magic or incantation) is evidenced by the drinking horns of Gallehus, which portray a variety of magical formulas, some of them in the shapes of humanoid figures in runic postures. Later Icelandic customs confirm this usage: for example, the teaching of the alphabet to young children by having them strike a posture that resembles a letter. All of these practices will be dealt with in detail in the practical portion of this book.

Another important use of the runes, which falls outside the scope of the present work, is that of divination. This topic is thoroughly treated in my *Runecaster's Handbook* (Weiser Books, 1988). The runic forms often were carved into pieces of wood, cast onto a white cloth, and then inter-preted according to strict criteria. The Roman historian Tacitus reports on this practice among the continental Germans in the first century CE.

All of the methods mentioned above are valid and extremely potent for magical purposes today. The runes and holy signs may be used as focal points for evocatory magic and meditation as well as self-transmutation and mystical communication. Runes are especially valu-able in magical works concerning victory, success, protection, rescue from restriction, love, and the gaining of wisdom.

The Runic Revival

Although many runic practices, and much rune lore, continued in a myriad of forms long after the coming of Christianity, the systematic transmission of the sacred rune lore belonging to the ancient vitkar and eriloz slowly disappeared. By the nineteenth century, only scattered pockets of "rune singers" remained in the remotest areas of Scandina-via. However, the runic mysteries are truly something indigenous to the innermost *selves* of many members of the Germanic tribes, and this "inner rune lore" could never be eliminated totally—it only retreated into the innermost shelters of the human soul, waiting to be reborn. Just as the gods and men retreat into abodes in the recesses of *Yggdrasill* (the world-tree) in order to survive the destructive powers released at *Ragnarök* (the destruction), so too did the runes hide themselves in the patterns of consciousness, awaiting the time when they might be reborn into a hospitable world that would again know their lore. As we read in the Eddic "Völuspá" (stanza 59) concerning the renewed world after Ragnarök:

> *Again the Æsir meet*
> *on Idha-plain,*
> *and speak of the mighty*
> *Midhgardh-serpent,*
> *and again remember*
> *the mighty World-doom*
> *and Fimbultýr's (=Ódhinn's)*
> *elder runes.*

The rebirth process of the runes has not been without pain and blood. Until now, it seems the vessels *were* as yet unfit to receive the wholeness of runic power because these vessels still contained wine made from foreign fruit. Leaders of the first half of the runic renaissance still contained many of the notions and prejudices of the Christian world in which they found themselves and in most cases they were unable to give up these notions. Therefore, they often incorporated these ideas into their runic systems. Sometimes this was done in an honest effort but in some cases it was done in the spirit of misguided manipulation of the sacred symbols.

At the dawn of the twentieth century the Pan-Germanic mystic Guido von List received a spontaneous runic initiation in which the "secrets of the runes" were revealed to him while he lay in darkness, his eyes bandaged for several months because of a cataract operation. From that time in 1902 to his death in 1919, List worked toward the restoration of what he called "*Armanentum.*" He formed the Guidovon-List-Gesellschaft (Guido von List Society) to support his investigations, and the Armanen Orden to carry out the esoteric functions of that society. List's aims often were political in nature (such as the unification of his native Austria and Germany), and his theories were to some degree based on the anti-Semitic dogma of the day. However, it is his runic theories that interest us here. List developed a magical runic system of eighteen runes (which we will call the *Armanen* system). This was based solely on the textual authority of the "Rune-Song" in the Eddic lay "Hávamál."

Although List never wrote about the magical runic practices employed by the Armanen Orden, the first book he produced after his "runic initiation" was entitled *Das Geheimnis der Runen* (*The Secret of the Runes*), which outlined his interpretation of the eighteen runes portrayed in this Eddic poem as well as his thoughts on a wide range of pertinent esoteric topics. This text has been translated as *Secret of the Runes* (1988). As it turns out this was the first in a series of works published between 1908 and his death in 1919. List maintained that the eighteen-rune system was the "primal" one, although there is no hard evidence other than the "Hávamál" to support his claim. The personal force of List and that of his extensive and influential Armanen Orden was able to shape the runic theories of German magicians (although not necessarily their *political* ones) from that time to the present day.

List's runic teachings later were incorporated into the racist *Germanen Orden*, which was one of the esoteric precursors of the National Socialist movement in Germany. His ideas also were further developed, and to some degree published, by two magicians, Siegfried Adolf Kummer and Friedrich Bernhard Marby, who developed a system of "runic yoga" or gymnastics that is worthy of study. Kummer and Marby are extremely important, since it is with their publications and experiments that the foundations of a practical and traditional system may be laid. But their ideas generally followed those of List and were not very traditional as far as the runes were concerned. They retained the Armanen system and further reinforced his racist ideas, as did another student, Rudolf John Gorsleben. Gorsleben's epochal work *Die Hoch-Zeit der Menschheil (The Zenith of Humanity)* is a huge compilation of rune lore based on the Armanen system. The early thirties seem to be the twilight of the first esoteric runic movement.

The year 1933 marks the beginning of the Nazi period and by 1935 the *Ahnenerbe* ("[Institute) for Ancestral Heritage") was formed by Heinrich Himmler around the ideas of historian and scholar of ancient religions and symbols Professor Hermann Wirth, among others. The runes formed an important part of Wirth's thinking, but we do not have many examples of practical applications of his ideas. During the Nazi regime all things "Germanic" were mobilized and directed toward politically manipulative ends. The runic forces themselves were used much less than some might have us believe. The *Ahnenerbe* and the *Totenkopf Orden* made more practical use of Judeo-Christian and virtually Manichean ideas in their magical traditions and organizational principles. The ideology of the ex-Cistercian monk Jörg Lanz von Liebenfels, embodied in his *Orden des Neuen Tempels* ONT), was most influential in this regard. One brief glance at a book on ancient Germanic and old Scandinavian culture and religion will show the massive degree to which the Nazis perverted the tribal systems of the ancients into a totalitarian imperial scheme. This was done basically through the "Christian camouflage technique"; that is, just as the Christian evangelists would employ old pagan symbols (such as the cross) to convert the heathens and then gradually infuse those venerable symbols with a contrary significance, so too did the Nazis employ old Germanic symbolism (which was very popular at that time) and infuse it with non-Germanic concepts for manipulative purposes. Runes and holy signs were abundant in the symbolism employed by the Nazi party, but it is not within the scope of this work to delve into this aspect of runic history.

The practical use of the runes as a system of magic (other than state controlled) and personal development virtually died out or was driven underground during the Nazi period. After the war the Armanen system was revived, and "reformed" by the German magician Karl Spiesberger. Spiesberger is a widely qualified, "eclectic" occultist who has authored books in the Hermetic as well as the runic tradition. His principal works on runic topics are *Runenmagie (Runic Magic)* and *Runenexerzitien für Jedermann (Runic Exercises for Everyone)*. In these books Spiesberger synthesizes the work of all the German runic magicians and experts who preceded him, within a pansophical framework. Although he eliminates all the racist and *volkisch* elements, he retains the *Armanen* system of runes, which by 1955 had become almost "traditional" in German circles. This system of eighteen runes forms a valid and working magical system, and the present work in traditional runic system(s) owes much to Spiesberger's research and synthesizing.

As valuable as Spiesberger's work is, it is still not a traditional form. Therefore, to some extent it is cut off from the innate powers slumbering in the ancient runes and their system. Whereas the Armanen system has a tradition dating only from around 1904 CE, the oldest runic evidence dates from about two thousand years earlier. Documents of the Viking and pre-Viking ages give us ample clues as to *how* the runes were used, but Spiesbergeris forced to neglect much of this material because it is the product of a different organic system. We *know* the elder tradition worked, and worked for hundreds of years, within well-developed cults. Therefore, it is certainly most fruitful to unlock the ancient runic treasure mounds that have stored the hoard of rune wisdom over the past millennia. But to do this, the psychic keys provided by the pioneering technical work done by the modern magicians in the Armanen traditions is extremely helpful.

Traditional Rune Lore and Ásatrú

The traditional runic systems are based on any of the three ancient futharks shown in Figures 1.3, 1.4, and 1.5. The magical system and cosmology presented here are found in the Elder Futhark of twenty-four signs. The rebirth of this lore is founded on a synthesis of the humane sciences of comparative religion, anthropology, archeology, and linguistics (known collectively as linguistic paleontology) and the methods of magic. This holistic[1] view also incorporates the natural sciences. Thus, the methods of traditional rune lore are founded in what is *known* of a magical system that was developed in days of yore. The hoary *eriloz* still speak to us through their runestones and through the mind runes (ON *hugrúnar*) they represent in our consciousnesses. This magical system was, however, only part of a much larger cosmological pattern that encompassed all the known and unknown worlds. For the ancient Germanic tribes magic, religion, and law—including social organization— were expressions of the same basic divine force. Therefore, in order for traditional magical forms to be truly reborn in Midhgardhr, a vessel for this holistic conception first had to be nurtured.

With the dawn of the eighth decade of this century, a northern wind blew through the world, allowing the venerable forms of magic, religion, and law to develop again in a syncretic reality. On May 16, 1973, the *Ásatrúarmenn* (those believing in or trusting in the Æsir) was founded in Iceland by Sveinbjörn Beinteinsson. Although there had been precursors to this event earlier in the decade, it represented the crystalizing nexus of the movement that has come to be known as either *Ásatrú* (the faith of the Æsir) or Odinism. At present three major groups seem to foster this syncretic view: the Ásatrúarmenn in Iceland, the Ásatrú Free Assembly in California, and the Odinic Rite in England. Over time these larger groups have evolved, disbanded, and reformed, and the whole movement is moving ever more toward highly localized or regionalized tribal organizations rather than large international organizations.

All such groups tend to maintain a healthy independence from one another—an independence that unfortunately has often devolved into polarized quasi-political frictions mirroring the worst aspects of our present mundane world. These organizations are primarily "religious" in orientation; all the tenets of this noble faith are too complex to enter into in this work. Besides, their general lack of dogmatism defies a quick synopsis, and any attempt at such would only do disservice to the remarkable breadth of religious expression and experience found within the perimeters of Ásatrú. However, let it be said that the efficiency of the magical system presented here can only be increased by an understanding of and adherence to the holistic principles of this faith, since this is the kind of atmosphere in which the rune lore was first practiced.

There exists a kind of "runic order" called *The Rune-Gild*, which has existed since 1979 and is now a world-wide organization. As in ancient times the runes brought people of various tribes and lineages together in the search for the mysteries, so many of the problems of cultural polarization present elsewhere tend not to be an issue in the Rune-Gild.

CHAPTER 2

LORE OF THE ELDER FUTHARK

I n this chapter, which consists of twenty-four sections, each section is a systematic attempt to impart a body of lore that surrounds each of the runes of the Elder Futhark. Information contained in these sections may be applied directly to magical practice, and the intellectual understanding arising from this lore will serve to increase the depth of ritual experience. Further amplifications of this rune lore may be obtained from the tables of correspondences printed as Appendix D.

Each section is headed by the standard runic form exemplified by the majority of runic inscriptions in the elder row along with its numerical value. The rune names in Proto-Germanic (a reconstructed common ancestor of all Germanic languages), Gothic, Old English, and Old Norse are provided, together with their Modern English translations. Alternate forms of the rune found in various inscriptions also are given, followed by the phonetic value of the rune. This preliminary table concludes with an esoteric interpretation of the name(s) and an ideographic interpretation of the runic form. The body of the runic commentary provides mythological and cosmological as well as magical material pertinent to the understanding of the mystery embodied by the rune in question. These commentaries are intended to be only partial, while touching on the major aspects of the mystery. They should serve as material for meditation and stimulus toward further work by all vitkar. A synopsis of the interpretation is given as a group of key words that serve as convenient vessels for containing the larger body of knowledge.

The last three divisions of each section consist of more technical material. The *galdr* is the root form of incantation (or if you will, mantra), which is the vibratory embodiment of the rune. This formula is invaluable to the rune vitki as a tool in all phases of rune magic, and together with the form, it is the principal medium through which the runic force finds expression. These formulas are very flexible and should be the subject of extensive experimentation by each vitki. The idea of creating galdrar out of consonant-vowel combinations, as will be seen in the sections on galdr attached to each rune below, is supported by data found in what is called "The First Grammatical Treatis." I discuss this in an article published in *Mainstays*. Because of limitation of space, the complex poetic galdrar of the Nordic tradition may not be entered into here. The simple sound formulas are the most basic and therefore perhaps most useful in self-designed ritual work. The *stödhur (sg. stadha)* presented in these sections are based on the methods of S. A. Kummer and F. B. Marby. They are quite effective and provide a powerful mode of literally incorporating the runic power into the body of the vitki, thus facilitating the assimilation or projection of these holy forces. The final division concerns the various uses of each individual rune for magical or mystical purposes. The lore of individual runes is the foundation of runecraft, from which their complex interactions spring. But it must be stressed that this lore is "open-ended." For talented and dedicated vitkar, there is no limit to the correspondences that can be integrated once the basics have been mastered and an understanding of the relative power contexts of each rune within the futhark paradigm has been reached.

1

F

Names: GMC *fehu*: mobile property, cattle
         GO *faíhu*: cattle, mobile property
         OE *feoh*: cattle, money
         ON *fé*: livestock, money, gold
Alternate forms: ᚹ ᚠ ᚦ
Phonetic value: *f*
Esoteric interpretation of name: mobile property; power.
Ideographic interpretation: the horns of bovine livestock.

Commentary

Fehu is the raw archetypal energy of motion and expansion in the multiverse. It is the force that flows from Muspellsheimr, the source of cosmic fire, from which Midhgardhr was produced (see I-rune). The F-rune is the all-encompassing and omnipresent power symbolized by the charging bovine herd and by wildfire. The cosmic fire of Muspellsheimr is instrumental in the creation of the world, but it is also the principal agent in its destruction of Ragnarök. The firegiant, Surtr, spreads the flames of destruction over the world, thus destroying all but those gods and men who are to survive or to be reborn in the renewed world on the Idha plain (the shining plain). It must be remembered that fehu is not the undifferentiated power of the cosmic fire of Muspellsheimr but rather the mystery of its eternal working eminently throughout the multiverse.

This rune rules the basic force of fertility.

The F-rune contains the mystery of both creation and destruction and the harmonious functioning of these two extremes, which leads to dynamic evolutionary force. Fehu is the rune of eternal becoming. Along with several other runes, this describes the holy process of birth-life-death-rebirth, or arising-being/becoming-passing-away toward new arising. More specifically, fehu is the archetypal force that gives impetus to this eternal process.

The F-rune is the essence of mobile power. This is evident from the most mundane meaning of its name: "money" or "cattle" (contrast O-rune). This root word originally meant mobile wealth or property, then was attached to the concept of livestock, which was the main mobile form of property known to the most ancient Germanic peoples. Later this term was used for "money," hence the modern English word "fee."

All in all, the F-rune defines a mobile form of power. In the psycho-magical realm this concept of mobile force is closely connected with the old Germanic idea of the *hamingja*. This is an aspect of the psychosomatic complex that may be best described as a mobile and transferable magical power. The hamingja (which is often translated by such concepts as "luck" and even "guardian spirit") may be sent forth from an individual in a manner akin to that of the "astral body" in other traditions. Fehu is the directed expansive force that facilitates the projection of soul entities and magical power from person to person, or from a person to an object.

Often the power of the F-rune is manifested in the mythology as an otherworldly glow around grave mounds and hills, or even as a ring of fire.

. . . .

Keywords:

Mobile force
Energy, fertility
Creation/Destruction
   (Becoming)

Galdr:

fehu fehu fehu
fffffffff
fu fa fi fe fo
of ef if af uf
fffffffff

. . . .

Stödhur:

Both arms slanted upward, the left being somewhat higher; fingers pointed for directing power, palms pointed out for drawing force. Face toward the sun.

. . . .

Magical workings:

1. Strengthens psychic powers.

2. Channel for power transference or projection; the sending rune.

3. Drawing the projected power of the sun, moon, and stars into the personal sphere.

4. Promotion of personal and social evolution.

5. Increase in personal monetary wealth.

2

ᚢ

Names: GMC *úruz*: the aurochs
        GO *úrus*: the aurochs
        OE *úr*: ox, bison
        ON *úr*: drizzle, rain
Alternate forms: ᚢ ᚢ ᚢ ᚢ ᚢ ᚢ
Phonetic values: *u, v*
Esoteric interpretation of names: aurochs—the primal fertilizing essence.
Ideographic interpretation: the horns of the aurochs, or falling drizzle.

Commentary

The U-rune is the mother of manifestation. In the mythology this is represented by the great cow Audhumla, which licked a great icy block of salt in order to form the primal androgyne Búri. Also, she was the source of sustenance for the cosmic giant Ymir. Audhumla was herself formed from the dripping rime produced when the world fire met the world ice. This is also the unmanifested energized essence from which the cosmic ice and Audhumla were originally formed.

Uruz is the patterning and formulating power in the multiverse, the source of the ordering principles that lead to the final formulation of the world. The U-rune is the unmanifested pattern of matter (contrast with the antimatter nature of *isa*).

This is the cosmic seed, the world force analogous to the *semen virile*.

It contains the mystery of the formulation of the self, a composite paradigm of all the aspects of the psychosomatic complex, just as the multiverse is framed from the various worlds. Uruz is the forming *force*, not the form itself (see the H-rune).

The U-rune is the shaping power that defines the origin and destiny of all things. This mystery may be demonstrated through the shape of the stave, as shown in Figure 2.1. Uruz is the eternal reservoir of archetypal patterning.

Because of its shaping power, uruz is a rune symbolizing wisdom and lore, as the pattern of preserved tradition that is sprung from the natural order. Just as this indicates a healthy society (one in accordance

Figure 2.1. U-rune pattern of manifestation. This pattern is essentially that of being drawn up into the time-space continuum until the force of the I -rune eventually draws it back to its source.

with natural order), so too is this a rune of good physical health in the personal realm. The U-rune promotes strong and harmonious organic systems. It is the rune of vital strength and virility.

. . . .

Keywords:	Galdr:
Archetypal patterning	uruz uruz uruz
Organic organization	uuuuuuuuuu
Wisdom	uuuuurrrrr
Health	uuuuuuuuuu
Vital strength	

. . . .

Stödhur:

Bend at the waist, with the back horizontal and parallel to the ground. Arms and finger tips point toward the ground; the head should be toward the east.

. . . .

Magical workings:

1. Shaping and forming circumstances creatively through will and inspiration.
2. Healing and maintenance of good mental and physical health.
3. Bringer of fortunate circumstances.
4. Induction of magnetic earth streams.
5. Realization of causality.
6. Knowledge and understanding of the self.

3

⟨ᚦ⟩

Names: GMC *thurisaz*: the strong one, giant
GO *thiuth*: the good one
OE *thorn*: thorn
ON *thurs*: giant

Alternate forms: þ ▷

Phonetic value: voiceless *th* as in "thorn"

Esoteric interpretation of name: Ása-Thárr, the enemy of unfriendly forces.

Ideographic interpretations: the hammer, or the thorn on a branch.

Commentary

Thurisaz is the directed cosmic force of destruction and defense. It is the archetypal instinctual will, without self-consciousness. The TH-rune is a symbol of lightning and thunder and is equated with Mjöllnir, the hammer of Thórr. This weapon is the destroyer of the etins and the protector of Midhgardhr and Ásgardhr. Thórr is in many ways similar to the giants *(thursar)* in his size and brute strength, and is therefore ideal as a counterforce to them. The Æsir constantly strive to maintain their enclosures in the multiverse, and the power of this rune is invaluable in this effort. The idea expressed by this aspect of thurisaz is identical with that of the hammer sign ⊥. This is the forward-thrusting force of destruction of powers hostile to cosmic order. These hostile powers are not morally "evil" in the Judeo-Christian sense of the word; they are merely detrimental to the established and instinctual life urge exemplified by the Æsir and Vanir and expressed in mankind. Just as the thorn protects the rose, so too does Mjöllnir protect Midhgardhr and Ásgardhr.

The TH-rune is the container of the life-death polarity. It is the ultimate power to assimilate potential energy of two extremes of kinetic energy into a pattern of action. Thurisaz is a projectable form of applied power. Generally, this may work as a limitation and direction of various energy-form binary pairs found throughout the rune row. That is, any rune that is essentially energetic (e.g., :ᚠ: :ᚲ: :ᚺ:) may be combined with any rune that has primarily paradigmatic characteristics (e.g., :ᚾ: :ᚹ: :ᛒ:) by the TH-rune force and directed in a real way.

Thurisaz is also a rune of regeneration and fertilization. As the lightning heralds the crop-bringing rains, so the TH-rune breaks down barriers and fecundates so that new beginnings may be made. The *thorn* is the thorn of awakening that dispels the power of the *svefnthorn* (sleep-thorn).

This is the cosmic phallic power.

. . . .

Keywords:

Force of destruction / defense
Action
Applied power
Direction of polarities
Regeneration (following
   destruction)

Galdr:

thurisaz thurisaz thurisaz
th th th th th th th th th th
thur thar thir ther thor
thu tha thi the tho
th th th th th th th th th th

. . . .

Stödhur:

Stand upright with the left arm bent at the elbow, hand on hip, with the palm grasping the hip bone. Face east or south.

. . . .

Magical workings:

1. Defense (active).

2. Destruction of enemies, curses.

3. Awakening of the will to action.

4. Preparedness for generation in all realms.

5. Love magic.

6. Knowledge of the division and unity of all things.

4

ᚠ

Names: GMC *ansuz:* a god, ancestral god
GO *ansus:* a runic god name
OE *ós:* a god
ON *áss:* a god, one of the Æsir
Alternate forms: ᚭ ᛆ ᚽ ᚠ
Phonetic value: *a* (*o* in the A-S row)
Esoteric interpretation of name: Ódhinn of the Æsir.
Ideographic interpretations: the wind-blown cloak of Ódhinn.

Commentary

Ansuz is the mysterium tremendum of the rune row.

The A-rune is instrumental in the creation of mankind. It describes two of the several spiritual gifts given to Askr and Embla (the primal man and woman) by the gods Ódhinn, Hœnir, and Lödhurr (a threefold aspect of the god Ódhinn). These gifts were *önd* or *anda* (breath, spirit, animating life principle) and *ödhr* (inspired mental activity, inspiration). This is the stave of Ódhinn as the numinous god of magic and of ecstasy.

Ansuz is the receiver-container/transformer-expresser of spiritual power and numinous knowledge. This force is received from the Æsir and transformed in humanity to be re-expressed toward the multiverse in magical and religious acts. This ecology of power works in tandem with that described by Ódhinn's reception of rune wisdom and subsequent expression of that wisdom to mankind. The A-rune encompasses the medium through which numinous knowledge is received, the container of that power, and the force itself, which is manifested as the ecstatic state. This container-contained equation is common for symbols of the inspired or ecstatic state. In Norse mythology the poetic mead of inspiration and the vessel in which it is contained are both known by the name Óthrœrir (the exciter of inspiration). This is the ecstasy that leads to the formation of a body of lore and wisdom.

This is the rune of the word, song, poetry, and magical incantation (galdr) as a container and expresser of magical force.

Ansuz is a magical ancestral power, one that has been handed down from generation to generation along genetic lines. The ancient Germanic peoples knew that they were "descended from their Gods," as the gene-alogies of their kings, heroes, and clanic chieftains show. The power link between gods and men was, for them, unbroken. It remains so. Through the power of this rune the realization of the link between the ancestral gods and their people may be regained. This is an ecstatic concept that complements the more stable, institutional force of *Othala*.

The A-rune embodies the death mysteries of the Æsir.

. . . .

Keywords:

Reception—transformation—
expression
Container / contained
Numinous knowledge
Inspiration
Ecstasy
Word-song
Death mysteries

Galdr:

ansuz ansuz ansuz
aaaaaaaa
aaaaaasssss
aaaaa
aaaaaaaaaa

. . . .

Stödhur:

Stand upright. Stretch out both arms parallel, pointing them down slightly, with the left arm lower than the right. Face north or east.

. . . .

Magical workings:

1. Increase of both active and passive magical powers and clairvoy-ant abilities, etc.
2. Convincing and magnetic speech, and the power of suggestion and hypnosis.
3. Acquisition of creative wisdom, inspiration, ecstasy, and divine communication.
4. Banishing of death and terror through knowledge of Ódhinn.

5

R

Names: GMC *raidho:* wagon
         GO *raidha:* wagon, ride
         OE *rádh:* a riding, way
         ON *reidh:* riding, chariot

Alternate forms: R R R

Phonetic value: *r*

Esoteric interpretation of name: the solar wagon, and the chariot of Thórr.

Ideographic interpretations: a wheel under the chariot ⊕ in the view ⚞⚟ as half of the solar wheel (see the S-rune).

Commentary

Raidho is the cosmic law of right and archetypal order in the multiverse. This is expressed by such natural phenomena as the daily path of the sun and the cycles of nature and humanity. The R-rune is the mystery of divine law, manifest in both the multiverse and in humanity.

Raidho came to be a symbol for organized religion, or better said, of Ásatrú, the ancient form of Germanic religion. In ancient times the external, self-conscious order of religion was much less *fixed* because of the internal, unconscious, and instinctual order of holiness. This internal order found expression in institutions that were a balanced blend of religion, magic, and law (politics). Today the R-rune is a symbol of the "way back to right," through the conscious efforts of *ásatrúarfólk* to recover the essence of the primal order.

This rune represents the right order of the initiate's journey through the paths of the Nine Worlds of Yggdrasill.

Good advice and judgment according to right are ascribed to raidho.

Another important aspect of the mystery of the R-rune is that of ritual; that is, arrangement of energy and actions according to a cosmic order for a specific purpose. Here the emphasis is on the right ordering of these energies.

Raidho is the channeling of force according to natural laws along the right road leading to the right result. It describes, and analyzes, a certain aspect necessary to the working of the laws of cause and effect (see also the P-rune).

The concept of rhythm and dance also are important to the R-rune. This rhythm is embodied in all the worlds of the multiverse. Through rhythmic action and ritual dance, the vitki may perceive and blend with the personal rhythm, and in turn become one with the world rhythm and dance. This is the rune of that rhythmic ritual dance, which still should be practiced today.

Raidho also may be expressed in the concept of spiral development. This is in accordance with the traditional ideology of the cycles of existence, ever in circles but always rising (or sinking) toward a goal—the point. Reaching this goal is not an end but a transformation and new beginning for another outward expansion.

In popular tradition it is a symbol for the Vehmic Court, and as such it is a sign of the deep indigenous religious laws of the folk having precedence over those of the civil authority.

. . . .

Keywords:	Galdr:
Right action and order	raidho raidho raidho
Cosmic cyclical law	rrrrrrrrr
Religion—magic	ru ra ri re ro
Ritual	rudh radh ridh redh rodh
Rhythm	(rut rat rit ret rot)
Journey	or er ir ar ur
	rrrrrrrrr

. . . .

Stödhur:

Stand straight, with the left arm bent at the elbow, palm on hip bone. The left leg should be slanted out, lifted off the ground; the right arm should be tightly at your side. Face south.

. . . .

Magical workings:

1. Strengthens ritual abilities and experience.

2. Access to "inner advice."

3. Raises consciousness to right and natural processes.

4. Blending with personal and world rhythms.

5. Obtaining justice according to right.

6

Names: GMC *kenaz:* torch
        GO *kusma:* swelling
        OE *cén:* torch
        ON: *kaun:* sore, boil

Alternate forms: ᚠ ᛦ ᚴ ᚫ ᛤ

Phonetic value: *k*

Esoteric interpretation of names: the controlled fire; cremation. The Gothic and Old Norse names are secondary—internal fire, inflammation, etc.

Ideographic interpretation: flame of the torch.

Commentary

The K-rune portrays the mystery of regeneration through death or sacrifice. This is the fire rune, that is, fire under human control in the form of the torch (as opposed to the more raw and archetypal power present in the F-rune).

Ritually, *kenaz* is the fire of creation, sacrifice, the hearth and the forge—fire controlled by mankind toward a willed result. Cremation as a funeral rite facilitates the transference of the psychic aspects of the psychosomatic complex to new and regenerated forms and prevents their return to the spent forms. The fire of the sacrifice cooks and makes the flesh of the sacrificial animal sacred and acceptable for consumption by men and gods. The fire is always viewed as a transforming and regenerating force.

Kenaz is the ability and the will to generate and create. Therefore, it is the rune of the artist and craftsman, and the technical aspects of magic. Again, the importance of controlled fire—controlled energy—is apparent. The controlled power of the psyche is combined with the controlled energy of nature, and this results in a crafted object. This is the "human rune," the rune of humankind.

A large amount of knowledge and technical lore is embodied in the K-rune, knowledge combined with ability.

The mystery of the creation of a third from the combination of two is also an aspect of kenaz. Opposites are bound together in an aesthetic fashion and the results of that union brought into manifestation.

The K-rune is the rune of human passion, lust, and sexual love—as *positive* attributes. This is the emotional root of creativity in all realms of action. The goddess Freyja finds many correspondences with this aspect of the rune.

Kenaz also is important to the concept *kin,* and especially to that part of clanic tradition that professes a unity of the living and dead members of the clan, existing in a syncretic form of conscious life force.

. . . .

Keywords:

Controlled energy

Ability

Transformation

Regeneration

Will to generate

Sexual lust

Creativity

Galdr:

kenaz kenaz kenaz

ku ka ki ke ko

kun kan kin ken kon

ok ek ik ak uk

kaunnnnnnnn

. . . .

Stödhur:

Stand upright with the right arm raised at a 45° angle, while the left arm is lowered by the same amount. The palm of the right hand faces outward, drawing power, while the fingers of the left hand are pointed, projecting into manifestation.

. . . .

Magical workings:

1. Strengthening of abilities in all realms.

2. Creative inspiration.

3. Higher polarization as a tool of operation.

4. Operations of regeneration, healing.

5. Love (especially sexual love).

7

$$\mathsf{X}$$

Names: GMC *gebo:* gift, hospitality
         GO *giba:* gift
         OE *gyfu:* gift, generosity
         ON *gipt:* gift, wedding (not in
         younger row)
Alternate forms: ᚠ ᛈ ᛞ ᚷ
Phonetic value: *g* as in "gift"
Esoteric interpretation of name: that which is exchanged between gods and men.
Ideographic interpretation: the crossing of two beams in the building of a structure; interaction of two forces.

Commentary

Gebo is the rune of "god," that is, the eminent unconscious magical force present in the Ginnungagap before the formation of the Worlds.[2] The holy mystery of the two (or many) in one.

It is the giver, the giving, the given, and that which is given to; "the subject, verb, direct object and indirect object of the multiverse." This also describes a part of the mystery of sacrifice as the gift (ultimately of power) that is given to mankind by the gods in order to maintain the ecology of cosmic power.

By the power of this rune persons are bound together through an act of will in order to affect a result. This stave symbolizes the root force of runic orders, the retinue system, etc.

The G-rune has some functional similarities to the A-rune, since it is also a rune of ecstasy. It is the mystery of ecstatic magical power that is perceived and retained by the vitki as numinous knowledge.

Gebo contains the secrets of psychically joining two people (usually male/female), or several persons, in order that they may produce a creative power greater than their sum total. This is the rune of sex magic. Sex magic was practiced in ancient Germanic times, especially for the acquisition of numinous knowledge and wisdom, Sigurdhr, the greatest of Germanic heroes, was initiated into runic wisdom by the *valkyrja* called *Sigrdrífa* (Brynhildr) in a ritualistic scene rich in sexual symbolism (a child is born from their union). This was the usual mode of sex magic in which energy was exchanged along the male/female polarity. Further evidence for this is provided by the eighteenth-rune stanza of the "Hávamál" (stanza 164):

> *That eighteenth I know,*
> *which I never reveal*
> *to maid or man's wife*
> *anything is better,*
> *than if one know it*
> *this leads to the last of the songs—*
> *but only for that one,*
> *who embraces me*
> *or that be my sister.*

Gebo is *the* rune of the brotherly or sisterly lover, and it is the psychosexual force exchanged between two poles of power—human to human, or divine to divine. In the latter case, gebo describes the sexual life force used in fertility magic and that used in shamanistic practices.

. . . .

Keywords:

Magical force

Giver; giving; given; given to

Ecstasy

Sacrifice

Sex magic

Galdr:

gebo gebo gebo

gu ga gi ge go

gub gab gib geb gob

og eg ig ag ug

g a a a a f f f f f f f

. . . .

Stödhur:

Stand with legs spread, feet straight, and knees locked. Arms are stretched out in an angle forming an X, with hands directly over feet.

. . . .

Magical Workings:

1. Sex magic.

2. Sex magical initiation.

3. Mystical union.

4. Increase in magical powers.

5. Harmony between brothers and sisters and lovers.

6. Magical influence in human and divine worlds.

7. Acquisition of wisdom.

---

8 ᚹ

Names: GMC *wunjo:* joy
          GO *winja:* pasture
          OE *wynn:* pleasure, delight
          ON *vend:* (a rune name) joy, hope (not in younger row)

Alternate forms: ᚹ ᚹ

Phonetic value: *w*

Esoteric interpretation of name: relationship of beings descended from same source.

Ideographic interpretation: the clanic or tribal banner, or weather vane.

Commentary

The W-rune is the root force of attraction that sympathetic beings (wights) have for one another, that is, wights descended from a common source. These beings are then bound together in an organic whole, which is exemplified in the world of men by the clan and tribe. In the ancient Germanic world, society was "clano-centric," for a strong traditional clan was the best protection against invaders from without or totalitarianism from within. By giving the honor and integrity of the clan first consideration the individual was best able to maintain his freedom

Wunjo is the mystery of the harmonious existence of varied affiliated forces. In the clan this is the source of the highest human joy. When all members of the clan are harmoniously working together, while integrated into their environment in a syncretic manner, a true state of holiness exists.

The power of the W-rune aids in the promotion of fellowship and goodwill between brothers and sisters, as such is a powerful force in the maintenance of societies and guilds.

Wunjo is the energy that binds different fields of force together and is therefore an invaluable concept to rune magic. With this energy the vitki can bind several runes into a single harmonious force that can work toward a specific result.

. . . .

Keywords:

Harmony

Well-being

Fellowship

Binding

Galdr:

wunjo wunjo wunjo

wu wa wi we wo

wun wan win wen won

wo we wi wa wu

wwwuuuunnnnn

. . . .

Stödhur:

Stand upright with legs together. Place the fingertips of the left hand on the crown of the head. Keep the right arm close at the side.

. . . .

Magical workings:

1. Strengthens links and bonds.

2. Invocation of fellowship and harmony.

3. Banishes alienation.

4. Happiness and well-being.

5. Realization of the links and multiplicity of relationships of all things.

6. Binding runes toward specific purposes (see bind runes, etc.).

9

ᚺ

Names: GMC *hagalaz:* hail, egg(?)
GO *hagl;* hail
OE *hægl:* hail
ON *hagall:* hail

Alternate forms: ᚺ ᛂ ᚺ ᚺ ᚺ ✳ ✢

Phonetic value: *h*

Esoteric interpretation of name: icy egg or seed of primal cosmic life and pattern.

Ideographic interpretations: the connection of two standing beams (realms of being) by a cross bar in half-timbered building technique (: H :) or the primal snowflake pattern (: ✳ :).

Commentary

Hagalaz is the cosmic ice egg that is filled with crystalized magical power and cosmic pattern. The hailstone is the symbol of the yeasty rime "egg" that contains the seed of Ymir, the primal rime-giant. Ymir was formed from the juncture of world fire of Muspellsheimr and world ice of Niflheimr. This is the complete potential multiversal paradigm—the egg of manifestation. This "seed" concept is emphasized in the Old Icelandic Rune Poem:

Hagall is a cold grain
and a shower of sleet and
a sickness of snakes

The H-rune is the mystery of the framework of the world, and defines the primal form of the multiverse. The snowflake forms itself along the sixfold pattern of the old holy sign : ✳ :, which came to replace : ᚺ : in the Younger Futhark.

Hagalaz is the complete model containing the potential energy of neutral power in the multiverse, which is born from the dynamic, generating, evolving unity of fire (energy) and ice (antimatter).

The H-rune describes the eternal cosmic harmony.

In Germanic religion and mythology, the number nine is the most sacred and mysterious of numbers: there are nine worlds in Yggdrasil, Óðhinn hung for nine nights on that tree to gain the runes, the god Heimdallr was born of nine mothers, and so on. This is the number of a completeness that leads to a birth of greater power and productivity.

Hagalaz is the rune mother; this is because of its numerical value and its shape, : ✳ : (which may indeed be the primary one). All the runic forms may be derived from the sixfold hagalaz when it is placed within a solid figure (see Figure 2.2).

The H-rune embodies ongoing evolution within a fixed framework.

Hagalaz is a stave of protection and banishment because its complete and harmonious nature promotes special security and prevents the intrusion of disharmonious elements.

Figure 2.2. The mother rune: the solid hagalaz.

Keywords:

Cosmic pattern, framework
Completion
Union (cosmic egg)
Evolution (within framework)
Protection

Galdr:

hagalaz hagalaz hagalaz
h h h h h h h h h h
hu ha hi he ho
hug hag hig heg hog
(hul hal hil hel hol)
oh eh ih ah uh
h h h h h h h h h h

Stöðhur:

I. Stand upright in a cross position with arms parallel to the ground and palms pointed outward.

II. This is a complete runic combination ritual of great power when properly performed.

1. Stand in cross position. Face north, take nine full inhalations, then turn with the sun (from north to east), and sing "hu ha hi he ho." Do this in all four directions, ending again in the north. This

exercise may be performed from the east during daylight hours or at sunrise.

2. N-rune stadha: nu na ni ne no (on first turn) hu ha hi he ho (on second)

3. E-rune stadha: e e e e e e e e e e (on first turn) hu ha hi he ho (on second)

4. I-rune stadha: i i i i i i i i i i (on first turn) hu ha hi he ho (on second)

5. M-rune stadha: m m m m m m m m m m (on first turn) hu ha hi he ho (on second)

6. T-rune stadha: Tiwaz Tiwaz Tiwaz (on first turn) hu ha hi he ho (on second)

7. G-rune stadha: gu ga gi ge go (on first turn) hu ha hi he ho (on second)

During the course of this exercise a total of 13 turns is made. Mentally take in no impressions during this operation; try to maintain an emptiness of consciousness. The exercise facilitates the workings of all the inner *hvel* (see section on stadhagaldr, p. 128).

. . . .

Magical workings:

1. Completeness and balance of power.

2. Mystical and numinous experience and knowledge.

3. Evolutionary, becoming operations.

4. Protection.

10

Names: GMC *naudhiz:* need, (fatalistic) compulsion
GO *nauths:* necessity, need
OE *nýd:* need, distress
ON *naudh(r):* distress, need, constraint

Alternate forms: ᚺ ᚻ

Phonetic value: *n*

Esoteric interpretation of name: need-fire and deliverance from distress.

Ideographic interpretation: the bore Ɩ and the bow ＼ that turns it to kindle the need-fire.

Commentary

Naudhiz is the cosmic force used by the powers that form the "fates" of mankind and the world. For an analysis of the Germanic concept of "fate" *(ørlög)* and these "shaping powers" *(Nornir)*, see the P-rune. The N-rune does not represent *ørlög;* rather it embodies a cosmic force necessary to its formulation, that of *resistance.* It is a synthesis of an implicit thesis and antithesis that is expressed throughout the rune row. Naudhiz is a two-pronged concept. It contains the idea of distress but also deliverance from that distress. This idea is well expressed in the pertinent stanza in the Old English Rune Poem:

> *(Need) constricts the heart,*
> *tho to the bairns of men it often becomes*
> *help and health nevertheless,*
> *if they heed it in time.*

The N-rune is the self-created fire, the need-fire, created by friction/resistance to serve the needs of man in the material as well as spiritual realms. Naudhiz is the will-directed action, with knowledge and wisdom, which may act as a counterforce to the often negative powers of *ørlög.* The motto for this rune provided by Guido von List sums up this aspect of the N-rune quite neatly: *Nütze dein Schicksal, widerstrebe ihm nicht!* ("Use thy destiny, do not strive against it!").

Naudhiz also represents the concept of stepping-forth-into-manifestation. This idea originated with the creation of the Nornir. At that time resistance was born in the universe, laws of causality went into action, and the seeds of the "destruction" of the world of the gods were sown. This must not be understood within the context of any type of "moral evil" or similar concepts. The holy Nornir also help sustain the multiverse by constantly pouring water from Urdhr's well onto the world-tree, so that it will not wither and die. Because of the sexual elements inherent in the symbolism of this stave, the N-rune became a powerful tool in Icelandic love magic. Also, it is a strong rune of protection—especially spiritual protection.

. . . .

Keywords:

Resistance

Distress

Deliverance (need-fire)

Stepping-forth-into-
manifestation

Galdr:

naudhiz naudhiz naudhiz

nnnnnnnnnn

nu na ni ne no

nudh nadh nidh nedh nodh

(nut nat nit net not)

un an in en on

nnnnnnnnnn

. . . .

Stödhur:

1. Stand erect, with the right arm raised to the side and the left arm slanting down to form a line with the right.
2. (a) Cross-stadha. Say "*æpandi nam*"; (b) after speaking the formula, lower your hands to your hips.

. . . .

Magical workings:

1. Overcoming distress or negative *ørlög*.
2. Development of magical will.
3. Development of "spiritual" powers.

4. Use of the force of "resistance" under will toward magical goals.

5. Sudden inspiration.

6. Eliminates hate and strife.

7. Creates a need for order.

8. Recognition of personal need.

9. Protection.

10. Love magic—to obtain a lover.

11. Divination.

ᛁᛁ

Names: GMC *isa:* ice
GO *eis:* ice
OE *is:* ice
ON: *íss:* ice
Alternate forms: ᛁ
Phonetic value: *i*
Esoteric meaning of name: primal matter / antimatter.
Ideographic interpretation: the icicle, or the primal ice stream / wave out of Niflheimr.

Commentary

The I-rune is the antipolar force to the F-rune. *Isa* is a world ice that flows forth from Niflheimr. It does not represent matter, but rather a concept of antimatter, which, when combined with the energy flowing from Muspellsheimr, leads to the formation of what *we* call "matter" (Midhgardhr). *Isa* may be equated in some cases with the *prima materia* of other philosophies. In many ways this mystery may be symbolized by the "black hole." The I-rune is the force of attraction, gravity, inertia, entropy in the multiverse. In mythology, aspects of this force are represented by the rime-giants (*hrímthursar*). Isa is a stillness and lack of vibration—a unique mystery in the Germanic cosmogony / cosmology. This concept is as metaphysical as that which is called "spirit."

Ice and fire are the forces through which the world is created, but they are also the forces that will bring "existence" to an end.

Isa is a symbol for the individual ego because of its centralizing and concentrating effect. It is a force that holds the ego-self together during the stressful trials of the initiation process, and as such it is a bridge between the worlds and over waters.

Keywords:

World ice

Antimatter

Concentration

Ego

Galdr:

isa isa isa

iiiiiiiiii

iiiiisssss

(sssss iiiii)

iiiiiiiiii

Stödhur:

1. Stand erect with arms tight against sides.
2. Stand erect with arms straight overhead, with the palms touching one another.

Magical workings:

1. Development of concentration and will.
2. Constriction, halting of unwanted dynamic forces.
3. Basic ego integration within a balanced multiversal system.
4. Power of control and constraint over other wights.

12

Names: GMC *jéra*: the (good) year, harvest
        GO *jér*: year
        OE *gér*: year
        ON *ár*: year, (good) season

Alternate forms: ᛃ ᛉ ᚻ ᛁ ᛕ ᛋ ᛏ ᛖ

Phonetic values: j (pronounced *y* as in "yard"). In the later ON period, after about 600 CE, the initial *j* was lost in the West Norse dialects and thereafter the rune stood for *a*.

Esoteric interpretation of name: life cycle, cycle of the sun.

Ideographic interpretation: the holy marriage of heaven ∧ and earth ∨, or the dynamic rotation of the summer-winter cycle.

Commentary

Jera embodies the cyclical pattern of the universe expressed in the formula arising-being/becoming-passing-away to new arising. This is a basic pattern working throughout the rune row. The J-rune is one of the two "central runes" in the scheme of the Elder Futhark, and it defines the cyclical nature of the ever-becoming horizontal plane. It is the secret of the omnipresent circumference.

This is the mystery of the twelve-fold cycle of the yearly solar cycle. Raidho is the daily path and guiding force of the sun, jera her yearly path, and *sowilo* the archetypal sun herself.

Jera is the reward for honorable, right, and lawful (natural) past action. This has no real moral implications—it is a natural law. If the sowing is done correctly, according to tradition, and "luck" (hamingja) is with you, then the reaping should be great. It is the fruition of efforts well spent toward a willed or instinctual goal. This is true and valid for the numinous as well as phenomenological realms.

The cosmic fertility aspect of this rune points to the Vanic god Freyr, who is invoked *til árs ok fridhar* (for good season [harvest] and peace).

The Old Norse name *ár* provides us with the popular association of this rune with the eagle (ON *ari*) as a symbol of the swift flight of the archetypal sun.

Keywords:

Cyclical development

Solar year cycle (12)

Reward

Fruition

Eagle

Galdr:

jera jera jera

jjjjeeeerrrraaaa

jjjjjjjjjj

ju ja ji je jo

(jur jar jir jer jor)

jjjjeeeerrrraaaa

Stödhur:

Stand upright with right arm bent so that the thumb of the right hand touches the crown of the head. The left arm is bent at the same angle with the fingertips of the left hand touching the left hip bone.

Magical workings:

1. Fertility, creativity.

2. Peace, harmony.

3. Enlightenment.

4. Realization of the cyclical nature of the multiverse.

5. Realization of the mystery of the omnipresent circumference.

6. Bringing other concepts into material manifestation.

13

Names: GMC *eihwaz* or *iwaz:* yew tree
GO *eihwas*: yew tree
OE *éoh:* yew tree, or eow: mountain ash
ON **ihwar:* yew (in runic inscriptions only)
It is not in the younger row in this form, but the Norse
Futhark has *ýr*: yew; bow of yew wood in the form ⅄.

Alternate forms: | ⅄ ⅄ ✳

Phonetic value: uncertain—somewhere between *e* and *i*. This rune stave is essentially a magical sign that occurs infrequently in the writing of words.

Esoteric interpretation of name: yew as the tree of life and death—the world-tree, Yggdrasill.

Ideographic interpretation: the vertical column of the multiversal tree.

Commentary

Eihwaz is the vertical axis of the world that defines the central column of Yggdrasill, the cosmic tree. The world-tree of the ancient Norse was in most cases actually symbolized by a yew tree, not an ash as often supposed. This idea is supported by the old texts, which always refer to its "evergreen "quality and its needles—the yew is a conifer. An alternate name for the yew in Old Norse is also *barraskr* (needle ash). The word *Yggdrasill* means either "Yggr's (Ódhinn's) steed," or "yew-column." The former meaning is a direct reference to the shamanistic ritual in the "Hávamál." The gallows often are poetically described as the "horse of the hanged" in Old Norse. This is the rite by which the *erifoz* fares to Hel (realm of the dead, or underworld) and thence to all Nine Worlds to gain their wisdom. This is accomplished along the vertical dimension of the multiverse. The : ⌁ : defines this "numinous axis" that pierces through and connects the three realms of heaven, earth, and the underworld. A similar, but distinct function is performed by the T-rune. There the emphasis is on *separation;* here, on *communication.*

This rune contains the mystery of life and death, and mystically unifies them in its essence. The yew *(Taxus baccata)* contains an alkaloid toxin that affects the central nervous system. Prepared properly, this is a powerful hallucinogen. A certain professor of medicine named Kukowka, at the University of Greiz in East Germany, discovered that on warm days the yew emits a gaseous toxin that lingers in the shade of the tree and may cause hallucinations for an individual under its branches. The importance of this discovery in the study of the shamanistic character of the Yggdrasill initiation should not be lost. Besides its association with death, the *yew* tree is also a symbol of eternal life and endurance. This is because of its "evergreen" nature and because it is an extremely long-lived (up to two thousand years) and hardy tree with exceptionally hard wood. The yew is often found in the old church graveyards of Europe— former sites of Ásatrú temples.

Eihwaz is a life-giving force and the mode by which that force is sustained.

In the younger row this rune is represented by : λ : (ON *ýr*) sometimes meaning "bow made of yew wood." This is because bows often were fashioned from the hard, resilient yew wood, and because of the connection of the "Bow God," Ullr, with the mystery of the yew. Ullr is the archaic death god who rules the season of Yule.

The yew is also a powerful stave of protection and banishing. (See also the form : Υ : and its connections in this regard.) Even today in certain parts of Germany the magical saying *Var den Eibm kann kein Zauber bleiben* (before the yews, no (evil) magic can remain) may be heard. We also have a preserved runic talisman that is an example of "yew magic." This is found on the stave of Britsum, carved in yew wood sometime between 500 and 650 CE. In the Frisian dialect, its inscription is interpreted as "Always carry this yew! Strength is contained in it!"

. . . .

Keywords:

Vertical cosmic axis

Numinous initiation

Life / death

Endurance

Protection

Galdr:

eihwaz eihwaz eihwaz

(iwaz iwaz iwaz)

e e e e e e e e e e

(a neutral, dosed vowel sound)

iwu iwa iwi iwe iwo

iwo iwe iwi iwa iwu

e e e e e e e e e e

Stödhur:

Stand upright and stretch both arms down at a 50° angle, while lifting the left (or right) leg back at an equal angle.

Magical workings:

1. Initiation into the wisdom of the World-Tree.
2. Realization of the death/life mystery and liberation from the fear of death.
3. Development of spiritual endurance and hard will.
4. Spiritual creativity and vision.
5. Protection from detrimental forces.
6. General increase in personal power.
7. Communication between levels of reality—the worlds of Yggdrasill.
8. Memories of former existences in the ancestral stream.

14

Names: GMC *perthro:* device for casting lots
GO *pairthra:* dice cup
OE *peordh:* chess man (?)
ON (not in Norse row, functions absorbed
by : ᚺ :, : ᛒ :, and : ᛉ :)

Alternate forms: ᚲ ᛰ

Phonetic value: *p*

Esoteric interpretation of name: divination as an indicator of *ørlög,*
the "primal laws."

Ideographic interpretation: dice cup; as a device used for casting lots.

Commentary

Perthro is a cultic symbol for the force of ørlög functioning throughout
the multiverse and the way in which men and gods may investigate its
workings. Ørlög is most often translated by the word "fate," but this
is much too simplistic and unfortunately loaded with connotations of
"predestination " and "predetermination" of the type found in Christian
dogma. This sense is totally lacking in the Norse term. Ørlög literally
means "primal layers"; that is, the layers (ON *log:* "laws") of past or former action indicated by the prefix *ør-,* which signifies the most primal or
basic form of something in time or space. These self-determined layers
of past action are the laws by which gods and men are governed. These
are not the immutable laws of nature but rather the immutable laws by
which the laws of wights are formed by past action and by precedent.
This cosmic principle is at the root of Germanic common law. Clearly,
it is a concept much akin to that expressed by the Sanskrit *karma* and is
contrary to the Judeo-Christian predestination.

It is not unlikely that the name, as mysterious as it has now become,
originally referred to a fruit-bearing tree of some kind, in contrast with
the evergreen eihwaz and that divinatory devices and staves were
carved from the wood of this tree.

The P-rune contains the mystery of the Nornic laws. The Nornir
are the medium through which action is received and transmuted into
a projectable but essentially unaltered form and returned to the sphere

from which that action was received. This is the rune of time, and this idea is also expressed by the Nornir. Their names are Urdhr, Verdhandi, and Skuld (Urdhr, "that which has become"; Verdhandi, "that which is becoming "; Skuld, "that which should become"—a non-past/present concept). Nornic force defines an aspect of the laws of cause and effect in the multiverse, and as such, an understanding of this force is indispensable in the working of runecraft.

The mystery of divination, and of synchronicity, is central to the P-rune. By the art of divination, the vitki is able to investigate personal or transpersonal ørlög and become aware of the Skuld-force as well as the influences of Urdhr and Verdhandi.

· Perthro is the great pattern of cosmic becoming, which should be understood according to the principles outlined above. It represents the paradigm along which resistance (: ↑ :) between forces is organically governed and balanced.

The P-rune is perceived as a constant change—that always remains the same.

. . . .

Keywords:

Ørlög

Time

Urdhr—Verdhandi—Skuld

Cause and effect

Evolution—change

Galdr:

perthro perthro perthro

pu pa pi pe po

purdh pardh pirdh perdh
pordh

po pe pi pa pu

peeeerrrthththththrrrroooo

. . . .

Stödhur:

Sit on ground with back straight. Bring knees up with feet flat on the ground. Rest elbows on knees with forearms slanted forward. Face west.

. . . .

Magical workings:

1. Perception of ørlög.

2. Divination.

3. Placing runic forces in the stream of Norni law.

4. To evolve ideas or events as a magical act.

15

ᛉ

Names: GMC *elhaz* or *algiz:* elk, protection
         GO *algis:* swan (?)
         OE *eolh:* elk
         ON **ihwar:* (in runic inscriptions only) yew, yew bow

Alternate forms: ᛉ ᛉ ᛦ

Phonetic value: a final grammatical *z*, which eventually developed into the final *r* of Old Norse.

Esoteric interpretation of name: protective force, *valkyrjur.*

Ideographic interpretation: the horns of the elk, the branches (and roots) of the tree, a swan in flight, or a splayed hand.

Commentary

This rune is historically perhaps the most complex of all from a symbological perspective. A unified ideological complex does rise to the surface once its secrets are penetrated.

The Proto-Germanic form *algiz* means "protection," and its stave form is perhaps derived from the basic sign of defense and protection: the splayed hand. The concept of the valkyrjur also has been connected to this stave through the interpretation of the name as "swan." The valkyrjur are protective, life-giving beings who often fly by means of magical cloaks made of swan feathers. These beings are protectors, power givers, and a mode by which Ódhinn communicates with his chosen heroes.

The sign : ᛉ : is often found carved into spears for protection and victory.

Elhaz, meaning "elk," refers to the four cosmic harts that constantly bite at the needles of the world-tree. The yew again comes into the symbol complex of this rune with the Old Norse word *i(h)war.* which occurs only in runic inscriptions. This term means either "yew tree" or "yew bow" and is later rendered by the word *ýr* and the stave form : ᛦ :. This form is an alternate of the usual : ᛉ : and in fact they are probably derived from a primal form : ᛉ : found in the Futhark of Charnay. This oldest form displays the tree symbolism quite graphically.

The Gothic word *alhs* (sanctuary) has been related to this rune as well. This is a protected grove or enclosure dedicated to the gods. The Z-rune contains an aspect of the protective power of the divine twins. Alcis, the name of the twins reported by Tacitus in the *Germania,* may indeed be related to the rune name. ideographically, the divine twins were sometimes represented as being joined at the head, rather like the primal form of the rune (see Figure 2.3).

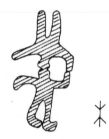

Figure 2 .3. Divine twins, from the rock carving of Ryland/Tanum.

In their aggressive, warlike aspect, the twins are visualized as harts, while in other aspects they are represented as horses (see E rune).

Elhaz is the power of human life and "spirit" striving toward the world of the Æsir.

It is the rune of the connection between gods and humanity, the force that draws the consciousness of man toward the realm of the gods. The Z-rune is the three-colored bridge of shimmering light, Bifröst, the "Rainbow Bridge" of Norse mythology. This bridge connects Ásgardhr, Midhgardhr, and Hel. It is another mode for the consciousness to traverse the worlds. It is the curved path of the branches and roots rather than the straight path of the trunk (: ᛏ :), a symbol of the magical power of the hamingja. The Z-rune is the force used by Heimdallr in his aspect as guardian of Ásgardhr. Elhaz is a rune of consciousness and awareness (a *hugrún).* It is over Bifröst that the rime- and fire-giants destroy the worlds of men and gods. All this is best understood through a synthesis of the diverse mysteries presented above.

The stödhur of the Z-rune are the traditional postures in which the Germanic peoples communicate with the gods (see the section of Stadhagaldr, see p. 128*).* Also, this shape was later employed as the M-rune in the Younger Futhark.

Keywords:

Protection-enclosure

Life

Bifröst

Path of the branches and roots

Connection between gods and
men

Galdr:

elhaz elhaz elhaz

z z z z z z z z z z (a deep
whirring, whistling sound)

uz az iz ez oz

oz ez iz az uz

zzzzzzzzzz

(mmmmmmmmmm)

Stödhur:

1. Stand upright with the arms stretched out upwards and to the sides.
2. Keep arm position the same as above, but kneel, sitting on the heels. Keep torso vertical with the head slightly tilted back.
3. Same arm position with the right knee on the ground and the left foot out in front with the thigh parallel to the ground.

Magical workings:

1. Protection, defense.
2. Mystical and religious communication with nonhuman sentient beings.
3. Communication with other worlds, especially Ásgardhr and the cosmic wells of Urdhr, Mimir, and Hvergelmir.
4. Strengthening of hamingja (magical power and "luck") and life force (see M-rune for more practical applications of the shape).

16

Names: GMC *sowilo:* sun
        GO *saugil:* sun
        OE *sigil:* sun
        ON *sól:* sun

Alternate forms: ᚼ ᛌ ᛎ ᚿ ᛔ ᛌ

Phonetic value: *s*

Esoteric interpretation of name: the holy solar wheel.

Ideographic interpretation: one part ᛌ of the dynamic solar wheel ᛋ, which developed with the form ⊕; or the thunderbolt.

Commentary

The S-rune is the archetypal sun and the light of that sun, symbolically expressed as the solar wheel. The concept of the turning wheel (ON *hvel*) is central to the understanding of the rune. This is represented as the wheels of the solar wagon : ᛉ : as well as the disk that is borne by that cosmic vehicular force. This symbol complex is the center of the ancient hyperborean sun cult, which was at its peak in the Bronze Age. The sun was known by two special names in the North. These are reflected in Old Norse *sól* and the cult word *sunna* (both feminine). In the "Alvíss-mal" (stanza 16) of the *Elder Edda* we read:

> It is called Sól among men
> and Sunna among the Gods.

Sól represents the phenomenon, while *sunna* is the noumenon, the spiritual power residing in the concept. The mystery of the sun is essentially a feminine one—the sun and solar power were considered feminine attributes by the ancient Germanic peoples.

Sowilo is the magical will that is active throughout the multiverse. Within the individual this will is expressed through the "spiritual wheels," the hvel. This word is an exact cognate to the Sanskrit *ćakra*. In this aspect it is a counterforce to the power of cosmic ice. The S-rune often has been connected to the power of the lightning bolt, and thus to the concepts embodied in thurisaz.

Sowilo is the eminent spiritual force that guides the vitki through the paths of Yggdrasill. It is an aspect of the goal, and also the active, willed path toward that goal. The S-rune may serve as a dynamic connection between heaven and earth (Ásgardhr and Midhgardhr). Sowilo is the rune of the Germanic code of honor, a powerful path to ecstatic experience.

In later times this rune became known as the "victory rune." Indeed, it is a potent, willed force. This can bring great success and victory to an individual when properly applied. But the true *sigrun* (victory rune) of the ancients was the T-rune.

. . . .

Keywords:

Solar wheel

Magical will

Guide

Goal and path

Success

Honor

Galdr:

sowilo sowilo sowilo

sssssssss

ssssoooollll

su sa si se so

(sul sal sil sel sol)

us as is es os

so se si sa su

sssssssss

. . . .

Stödhur:

1. Squat so that the calves and thighs are pressed together along their entire length, with the buttocks resting on the heels. Keep the torso vertical, with the arms along the sides of the thighs.

2. Standing with the body in the form of the S-rune, angle the arms along the sides of the body while the joints of the hips and knees form the : ↳ : rune.

These stödhur are reflected by an Old Norse term *knesol* (knee-sun) which describes the S-rune.

. . . .

Magical workings:

1. Strengthening of the psychic centers, hvel.

2. Increase in spiritual will.

3. Guidance through the pathways, "enlightenment."

4. Victory and success through individual will.

17

Names: GMC *tiwaz:* the god Týr
GO *teiws:* the god Týr
OE *tir:* the god Týr (OE Tiw), glory
ON Týr: the god Týr

Alternate forms: ↑ T

Phonetic value: *t*

Esoteric interpretation of name: the sky god.

Ideographic interpretation: the vault of the heavens ∧ held up by the universal column |, and sometimes the spear point.

Commentary

The T-rune embodies the force ruled by the god Ása-Týr. *Týr* is the Norse god of law and justice, who governs proceedings at the *thing* (the Germanic general assembly). The Týr force is one of passive regulation. In northern mythology, it is this god who comes closest to a transcendental quality. These characteristics are exemplified by the major Týr myth in which the god sacrifices his hand ("active abilities") between the jaws of the Fenris wolf in order to save his fellow Æsir from destruction. Thus, *tiwaz* is the rune of self-sacrifice and of kings and great leaders of the people.

The word *tiwaz, týr* in Old Norse, is the exact cognate to Sanskrit *dayus,* Greek Zeus, and Latin *Ju-piter.* A threefold mystery is contained in *tiwaz:* (1) justice, (2) war, and (3) world-column. Certain aspects of all three concepts are intimately related in the runic cosmology. Tiwaz is principally the force of divine order in the multiverse, and especially among mankind. But Týr is also important as a "war god." This is because of the special judicial and spiritual qualities that were imparted to conflict by the ancient Northmen. An Old Norse word sums up this aspect quite well: *vápnadómr* ("judgment by arms": war). Combat was seen as a struggle between numinous forces in conjunction with physical ones. Both of these are considered to be extensions of the same ultimate source. The man, or army, with the most numinous power (which is developed by right and honorable past action) will be favored by ørlög to win the struggle. Týr rules over the administration of this form of justice, so he is invoked for victory and is therefore an important war god. The aspect of the world-column expressed by the T-rune is that of the separator of heaven and earth. This separation creates a phenomenological quality, and is therefore necessary to multiversal manifestation as we know it. This column maintains world order, and protects humanity and the gods from the destruction that would come should the heavens (energy) and earth (matter) collapse into one another.

Figure 2.4. The Irminsul of the Saxons.

Tiwaz is represented by the Irminsul of the Saxons (Figure 2.4). This world-column is the *axis mundi* and has its heavenly termination in the pole star.

The T-rune is the mystery of spiritual discipline and faith according to divine law. It is the religious instinct in the individual and society.

Tiwaz facilitates social integration and regulation according to the spiritual code of the Æsir.

. . . .

Keywords:

Justice

World order

Victory (according to law)

Self-sacrifice

Spiritual discipline

Galdr:

tiwaz tiwaz tiwaz

tiiiiirrrrr

tu ta ti te to

tur tar tir ter tor

ot et it at ut

(Týr Týr)

Tiiiiirrrrr

. . . .

Stödhur:

Stand straight, arms slanted down and away from the body in the form of the stave. Palms face the ground, although you may also experiment with the palms up.

This stödhur was developed as a bind rune of : ᚺ : and : ↑ :, and is popularly known as the Sig-Týr rune. It embodies the combined forces of these two powerful symbols. The galdr "Sig-Týr Sig-Týr Sig-Týr" should be used when invoking its force.

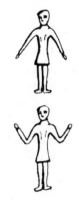

Magical workings:

1. Obtaining just victory and success.
2. Building spiritual will.
3. Develops the power of *positive* self-sacrifice.
4. Develops the "force of faith" in magic and religion.

18

Names: GMC *berkano:* birch goddess
GO *baírkan:* birch twig
OE *beorc:* birch tree
ON *bjarkan:* runic birch goddess (from
ON *björk:* birch)

Alternate forms: ᛒ Β Ᏼ |ϟ

Phonetic value: *b*

Esoteric interpretation of name: the numen of the birch as earth mother.

Ideographic interpretation: breasts of the earth mother ⚠.

Commentary

The B-rune contains the complex mystery of the great mother. In its cosmological aspect it is the mother of all manifestation and embodies the mysteries of cosmic and human birth and rebirth.

Berkano rules over the four pivotal human "rites of passage," which take place at the crucial times of birth, adolescence, marriage, and death. This birch goddess also displays the darker side of the "Terrible Mother," ruling over death. In Norse mythology she is represented by Hel. In the *Germania*, chapter 40, Tacitus reports on the goddess Nerthus as the earth mother. In this cult, the goddess is attended by a priest and she is drawn throughout the territory in her chariot, spreading her blessings of peace and fertility. When the procession is at an end, Nerthus receives human sacrifice in order to replenish her spent power.

The B-rune is the container of all becoming/being. It is the unity of the birth-life-death-rebirth cycle through the "mystery of the moment." This is the "unit of evolution," that moment of "being" (a single complete cycle of arising-being/becoming-passing-away to new arising) from which "becoming" is built. The phenomenon of chance in nature is described by this rune, because each moment each of these units of existence has its own uniqueness, although they are all held together by a universal pattern.

Berkano is the passive receptor and the conserving protective force. It conceals and protects. The B-rune rules over all protective or concealing enclosures such as caves, lodges, or the initiatory "earth houses" (ON *jardhhús*).

. . . .

Keywords:

Earth mother
Birth
Birth-life-death cycle
Containment
Moment

Galdr:

berkano berkano berkano
bu ba bi be bo
b e e e e e r r r r r
(burk bark birk berk bork)
ob eb ib ab ub
b e e e e e r r r r r

. . . .

Stödhur:

Stand erect with the left arm bent at the elbow, the palm resting on the hip. The left leg is bent at the knee with the heels touching. The left foot is set at a 90° angle to the right foot. The elbow and knee form the angles of the B-rune.

. . . .

Magical workings:

1. Rebirth in the spirit.
2. Strengthens the power of secrecy.
3. Works of concealment and protection.
4. To contain and hold other powers together.
5. Realization of the oneness of the moment as the mother of all things.
6. Bringing ideas to fruition in the creative process.

19 ᛖ

Names: GMC *ehwaz*: horse, or *ehwo*: the two horses
GO *aíhws*: stallion
OE *eh*: war horse
ON *íor*: horse (used only in cultic contexts, and not found in the Younger Futhark)

Alternate forms: ᚢ ᚾ

Phonetic value: e

Esoteric interpretation of name: the twin gods or heroes in equine aspect.

Ideographic interpretation: two upright poles bound together to symbolize the divine twins (the Bronze Age symbol  represented these divinities); also, the sign of two horses facing one another.

Commentary

Ehwo represents the power of the twin gods. This power construct is a reflection of a dual form of Germanic kingship. These leaders often were represented mythically as horses. Here we think of Hengist (stallion) and Horsa (horse), the Saxon conquerors of Britain. Also, the name of the twin gods of the Veda, the Aśvinau, literally means "the *two* horses." The harmonious relationship between the two forces represented in the dual construct is emphasized, rather than the defensive and outwardly directed power expressed in the Z-rune. All this points to the close relationship between man and horse felt by the Indo-Europeans in general and the Germanic peoples in particular. The horse is a source of numinous knowledge, and horses often were consulted by the ancient Germanic priests in divinatory rites.

The ehwaz is a spiritual quality closely connected to mankind *(mannaz)*. In Old Norse it is said: *marr er marins fylgia* (the horse is a man 's fetch). The bind rune of : ᛖ : and : ᛗ : is : ᛖᛗ : (em), which means "I am."

The E-rune facilitates the journey between the worlds of Yggdrasill—the vikti may literally ride its power through the realms of reality. Ehwaz is the rune of Sleipnir, Ódhinn's eight-legged steed. Many runic talismans portray a man riding a horse as a symbol form for integrated magical protection, under the rulership of Ódhinn. This is the otherworldly aspect of ehwaz, but the horse also is connected with fertility magic, and thus to Freyr, the god of fertility, peace, and sensuality.

This is a rune of trust and loyalty. The spiritual relationship that a horseman develops for his horse is a good illustration of the might of this rune. There is much power to be gained in this secret.

Ehwaz is the combination of *two* sympathetic, yet dually arrayed forces or entities (such as man/horse, horse/chariot, *man/fylgja*, body/soul) that work harmoniously together toward one goal (see the TH-rune for the contrasting concept).

The E-rune is the symbol of the ideal man-woman relationship and thus is the mystery of lawful marriage.

. . . .

Keywords:

Harmonious duality

Vehicle of otherworldly
   journeys

Fertility

Trust, loyalty

Legal marriage

Galdr:

ehwo ehwo ehwo

eeeehwooooo

ehwu ehwa ehwi ehwe ehwo

ehwo ehwe ehwi ehwa ehwu

eeeehwooooo

(Also experiment with the
   singular form *ehwaz*)

. . . .

Stödhur:

1. Stand straight with both arms slanted, the left pointed upward and the right downward to form the alternate form of the E-rune : ᛉ :
2. Also experiment with the E-rune bind-stödhur in which two vitkar, usually male and female, stand facing one another, each in the L-rune position, thus forming the E-rune : ᛖ :.

Magical workings:

1. Facilitation of "soul travel" throughout the worlds and projection of the "soul" in Midhgardhr.
2. Realization of fundamental unity of the psychosomatic complex.
3. Imparts trust and loyalty.
4. A source of prophetic wisdom.
5. Projection of magical power.
6. Facilitates swiftness in every regard.

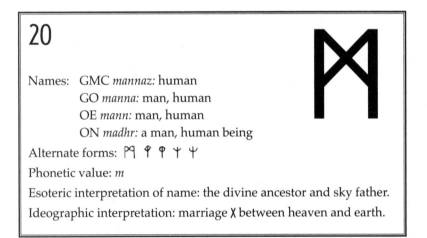

20

Names: GMC *mannaz:* human
GO *manna:* man, human
OE *mann:* man, human
ON *madhr:* a man, human being

Alternate forms: ᛗ ᛘ ᛙ ᛚ ᛛ

Phonetic value: *m*

Esoteric interpretation of name: the divine ancestor and sky father.

Ideographic interpretation: marriage ᚷ between heaven and earth.

Commentary

Mannaz is the mystery of the divine (archetypal) structure in every individual and in mankind in general. This structure is imparted by the god Heimdallr as the progenitor of mankind. This is described in the "Rígsthula" of the *Elder Edda*. In this poem it is told how Rígr (Heimdallr) engendered the archetypal members of the three social functions in the world of men—the Provider, the Warrior, and the Priest-King—which reflect the three levels of the divine structure. Heimdallr is indeed Ódhinn in one of his many guises, that of the All-Father (Alfadhir).

The M-rune is the symbol of Heimdallr as the genetic link between the gods and men, and as the guardian of Bifröst.

This is the rune that describes the Germanic peoples as being descended from their divine order and defines mankind as the progeny of the gods. It is the mystery of humanity and represents the runic structure in the soul of man.

Mannaz is the power of human intelligence, rationality, memory, and tradition.

It is the stave of the "perfected man"—the complete human being—an initiate in one of the many cults of the Elder Faith. Mannaz is an androgynous archetypal being, and therefore the mystery is one that embodies the power of the androgyne in the psychological sphere of humanity.

The M-rune stands for the institution of blood brotherhood.

. . . .

Keywords:

Divine structure

Divine link

Intelligence

Androgyne

Initiate

Galdr:

mannaz mannaz mannaz

mmmmmaaaaannnnn

mu ma mi me mo

mun man min men mon

um am im em om

mon men min man mun

mmmmmmaaaaannnnn

mmmmmmmmmm

. . . .

Stödhur:

1. Stand erect with elbows lifted straight up and fore-arms crossed in front of the face or behind the head.

2. Use the elder Z-rune stadha, which is used as the younger M-stave Ⱦ *madhr*.

In both cases the stadha will increase the power of the head (hvel).

. . . .

Magical workings:

1. Realization of the divine structure in mankind.

2. Increase in intelligence, memory, and mental powers generally

3. Balancing the "poles of personality."

4. Unlocking the *hugauga,* the "mind's eye."

```
Names:   GMC laguz: a body of water
           (or laukaz: leek)
         GO lagus: water
         OE lagu: sea, water
         ON lögr: sea, water (or laukr: leek)
Alternate forms: ᚱ  ᚴ
Phonetic value: l
Esoteric interpretation of names: life energy and organic growth.
Ideographic interpretation: a wave, or the quick growing green
portion of the leek.
```

Commentary

Laguz is the basic life energy in the multiverse and the secret source of all organic life. Laguz is the law (ON *lög*) of life, throughout all the multiverse as well as in Midhgardhr. These are the layers (laws) of past cosmic and human action that govern the future development of life forms.

The L-rune represents the primal waters in Niflheimr that contain the latent, amorphous potential of life, which must be solidified as ice and energized by the fire of Muspellsheimr before the potential can be actualized in manifested pattern.

This is a potent rune of initiation—especially the initiation into life. In heathen times a newborn child was sprinkled with water and given its name, after it had shown itself worthy of life. This reintegrated the child into the life force of its clan. The mystery of *vat ni ausa* (the ritual of sprinkling with water) predates Christian influence and is a feature of the ancient Nordic doctrine of rebirth—*aptrburdhr*. The functions of the U- and L-runes are closely interrelated on different levels.

Laguz also includes the watery rite of passage at the end of life—the crossing of the primeval waters to the realm of the dead. The myths of Ódhinn as the ferryman of the souls are important in this regard. The ship burials of the Vikings and the symbolic water crossing indicated by them also are illustrative of this belief.

The form *laukaz* also means "leek," which is expressed in the Old Norse rune name *laukr*. This is a symbol of organic growth, phallic power (virtue), and fertility in the physical as well as spiritual realms. The L-rune rules over the lore of herbal magic, known in Old Norse as *lyf* and in Old English as *lac-nunga*. The *ítrlaukr* (shining leek) was often given to a young man once he had proved himself as a warrior.

. . . .

Keywords:

Life

Primal water

Passage to and from life

Growth

Vital power

Galdr:

laguz laguz laguz

llllllllll

lu la li le lo

(lug lag lig leg log)

ul al li el ol

lo le li la lu

lllllaaaaaguuuuu

llllllllll

. . . .

Stödhur:

Stand erect with both arms stretched straight out in front of the chest, slanted downward. The palms point to the ground. Practice also with palms pointed up.

. . . .

Magical workings:

1. Guidance through difficult initiatory tests.
2. Increase in vitality and life force.
3. Gathering of amorphous magical power for formation and structuring by the will.
4. Increase in "magnetism."
5. Development of "second sight."

22

Names: GMC *ingwaz:* the god Ing
          GO *enguz* or *iggws:* the god Ing, a man
          OE *Ing:* the god or hero Ing
          ON *Ing* or *Yngvi:* the god Ing (later a name of Freyr)
Alternate forms: ⋈ ⛢ ◇ ▢
Phonetic value: *ng* as in "long"
Esoteric interpretation of name: the earth god.
Ideographic interpretation: ⛢—the male genitalia; ◇—
the castrated male.

Commentary

Ingwaz is considered to be the name of an old Germanic earth god, who works in tandem with the earth mother, Nerthus. Their cult was most developed in ancient times in the North Sea regions. The Old English Rune Poem tells us:

> *Ing was at first*
> *among the East-Danes*
> *seen by men,*
> *until he went eastward over the wave,*
> *his wain rolled after him:*
> *thus the Heardings*
> *named the hero.*

The wagon or chariot mentioned is the same used in the Nerthus cult. Ingwaz represents the male consort of the earth mother, and the priest who attends her. So strong was this cult among the peoples of the North Sea that they were often referred to as Ingvaeones (those of Ing).

The Vanic god Freyr also was known as Yngvi, and he too took part in fertility rites in which he rode in a wagon in ritual processions. Freyr seems generally to have usurped the role and the name of Ing in the North.

In the Ing-Nerthus cult the female element consumes the male to replenish her powers after spending them giving fertility to the land and people. Here there are strong overtones of a Cybele-Attis type of cult.

The myth of Freyr giving up his sword to gain Gerdhr or the Ódhinic name Gelding (castrated horse), may be illustrative here. The male element represents the self-replenishing "cosmic food" of potential energy, which is held through winter by the goddess to be suddenly and violently released again in spring during the orgiastic processional ritual.

The NG-rune is a storehouse of potential energy that must undergo a gestation period in order to gain in strength. This is a principle that works on all levels of the multiverse, and it is a mighty rune of magic, for all power must undergo such a protected gestation period before it may be manifested in its most potent form.

One of the great secrets of Nordic sex magic is embodied in this rune.

. . . .

Keywords:

Potential energy
Gestation

Galdr:

ingwaz ingwaz ingwaz
iiiiinnnnnggggg
u ng ang ing eng ong
ong eng ing ang ung
iiiiinnnnnggggg

. . . .

Stödhur:

1. Stand straight with fingertips touching well overhead and elbows angled in the form of the stave.

2. Stand erect with fingertips touching just above the genitals with elbows forming the angles of the NG-rune.

. . . .

Magical workings:

1. Storage and transformation of power for ritual use.

2. Fertility rites.

3. Passive meditation and centering of energy and thought.

4. Sudden release of energy.

23

Names: GMC *dagaz*: day
       GO *dags*: day
       OE *dæg*: day
       ON *dagr*: day (not in younger row)
Alternate forms: ᛞ ᛝ
Phonetic values: g and voiced *th* as in "then."
Esoteric interpretation of name: the light of day.
Ideographic interpretation: the balance between night and day.

Commentary

Dagaz is the light of day, perceived at the moments of sunrise and sunset, dawn and twilight. It is the rune of total awakening. The mystery of this rune is expressed in the invocatory verses spoken by Sigrddfa when she is awakened from a magical slumber by the hero Sigurdhr ("the warder of victory"):

> *Hail Day!*
> *Hail to Day's sons!*
> *Hail Night and her daughter!*
> *Look upon us twain*
> *with loving eyes*
> *and give those sitting here speed!*
> *Hail the Gods!*
> *Hail the Goddesses!*
> *Hail the much needed earth!*
> *Sayings and sage wit*
> *give to us, the storied ones,*
> *and healing hands in this life!*
>
>   (*Poetic Edda* "Sigrdifumal" stanzas 2–3)

The D-rune represents the ritual fire of the hearth and the mystic light perceived by the vitki in magical operations.

Dagaz is the synthesis of the powers of day and night through the concepts of dawn and twilight. This is expressed by the heavenly phenomena of the morning and evening stars—as symbols of the divine twins.

This is the rune of polarity and of the "Ódhinic paradox," which is the central mystery of the Ódhinic cult. It is embodied in the paradoxical nature of the god Ódhinn himself and is best explained in terms of the "mystical moment." This is the moment that is sought out and that is found in the vortex of polarized concepts. These concepts are syncretized through a secret "alchemy" in which two extremes become one. Dagaz is that time/place in which darkness and light, pleasure and pain, life and death, body and soul, matter and energy are synthesized into a common concept that goes beyond their *perceived* opposition. In dagaz, language fails.

. . . .

Keywords:

Light Polarity

Syncretization

"Ódhinic paradox"

Galdr:

dagaz dagaz daga

dhdhdhdhdhdhdhdhdhdh

daaaaaagaaaazzzz

du da di de do

dh dh dh dh dh

odh edh idh adh udh

od ed id ad ud

daaaaagaaaazzzz

. . . .

Stödhur:

Stand straight and cross arms in front of the chest in a D-rune form, with the fingertips touching the shoulders.

. . . .

Magical workings:

1. Attaining mystical moment through penetration of the secret of the Ódhinic paradox.
2. Reception of mystical inspiration— the gift of Ódhinn.

24

Names: GMC *othala:* ancestral property
　　　　GO *othal:* property
　　　　OE *éthel:* hsomeland, property
　　　　ON *ódhal:* nature, inborn quality, property
　　　　　　(not in younger row)
Alternate forms: ᛡ ᛚ ᚱ
Phonetic value: *o*
Esoteric interpretation of name: immobile hereditary property.
Ideographic interpretation: enclosed estate dynamically-interacting with the environment.

Commentary

The mystery of *othala* is symbolized by the stronghold enclosure of the clan, which defines its holy boundary and serves to defend it against the unholy intruders. It is the essence of the cosmic concept of Midhgardhr—the enclosure in the middle.

The O-rune also is a sign of inborn qualities that are the result of descent from a certain clan or tribe. This is essentially spiritual in origin and is ultimately derived from the divine ancestry plus past action of the ancestors. Othala is the mystery of the fylgja as a spiritual source of magical power, which results from the virtuous deeds of past generations as runic imprints into the "genetic codes" of the descendants—a powerful rune of Ódhinn. The stave form : ᛟ : serves as a monogram of Ódhinn.

It is a symbol of that which is inherited through the generations by the whole clan in both the material and spiritual realms. It is as immovable as the land and cannot be transferred out of the clan/tribe. However, through the institution of marriage those outside the clan have access to its power through integration with it. Othala is the wise and just management of the land by the noble ones: those possessed of the spiritual power of this rune in accordance with clanic tradition and law.

This is the rune of material prosperity and well-being. It works together with the complementary concept of mobile property—power contained in the F-rune to develop and maintain this important quality in the multiverse. Othala is the rune that provides human liberty in a secure and lawful society, integrated with itself and with its environment. It is preserved clanic and tribal law on a spiritual level. In Ásatrú this rune is expressed by the kindred.

....

Keywords:	Galdr:
Sacred enclosure	othala othala othala
Inherited power	oooooooooo
Preserved freedom	ooooo
Prosperity	othul othal othil othel othol
	othol othel othil othal othul
	ooooo

....

Stödhur:

I. Stand with legs spread wide, as in the G-rune stadha. and arms in the second NG-rune stadha, with fingertips touching just above the genitals. This is effective in operations to bring the will of the vitki into manifestation.

II. Again, stand with legs spread, but with the arms in the first NG-rune stadha. with fingertips touching well overhead. This stadha is most effective in works of inspirational intent.

....

Magical workings:

1. Maintaining order among fellows.
2. Concentration on common interests in home and family.
3. Shift from ego-centricity to clano-centricity.
4. Collection of numinous power and knowledge from past generations.
5. Acquisition of wealth and prosperity.

CHAPTER 3

THEORY OF RUNE MAGIC

I t is not possible in a book of this scope to present all levels of the runic cosmogony and cosmology. Certain portions of this lore have been used in interpreting and illustrating the properties of the individual runes, and before progressing to the theories of rune magic proper, steps should be taken to explain the cosmos in which these mysteries manifest themselves.

The Rune World

The best source for understanding the runic cosmology is found in the Eddas, where we read that before time began there was Ginnungagap, which literally means a "magically charged void." In the southern extreme of this void there appeared a world of fire called Muspellsheimr, and in the North arose Niflheimr or the "mist world." From Niflheimr came yeasty waves of ice until the northern region of Ginnungagap became filled with this icy rime and drizzle. At the same time the fire of Muspellsheimr spewed forth sparks and glowing particles. But the center remained "mild as windless air." When the forces of fire and ice met, the ice was melted and the yeast was quickened by the power of Muspellsheimr. This formed the primal giant Ymir ("the roarer"), which indicates "primal vibration." From this androgynous being sprang the races of rime-giants.

Ymir was fed by the milk of Audhumla, the cosmic cow, which was instantly formed from the dripping rime. She licked salty ice blocks and thereby formed the archetypal man, Búri, also an androgynous being. From Búri sprang Borr who married Bestla, the daughter of a rime-giant. From this union Ódhinn, Vili, and Vé (masters of inspiration, will, and holiness, respectively) were born. They slew Ymir and fashioned and fitted the world with portions of his cosmic body. The sons of Borr then fashioned the primal man and woman, called Askr and Embla ("ash" and "elm"). The gods gave them a variety of "spiritual" gifts, which will be discussed below in the section on the aspects of the soul and magic.

The intricacies of the elegant and complex runic cosmology cannot be entered into here, but what is important to note is that (1) there is no personal *Creator:* cosmogony is seen as a natural and organic process; (2) the universe ultimately derives from a *single* source, Ginnungagap, which divides itself into *two* extremes of fire (expansive energy) and ice (primal matter/antimatter). This polarity is mutually attracted, and from their (re)union the primal essence and archetypal pattern for manifestation are formed. From this framework the multiplicity of being evolves.

The Eddas teach us that once "creation" had been stabilized, the multiverse consisted of nine worlds, contained in and supported by the world-tree, Yggdrasill. These worlds contain countless abodes and dwellings. In the center is Midhgardhr, with the other worlds arrayed around, above, and below it. In the north in Niflheimr; in the east, Jotunheimr (Etin-world); in the south, Muspellsheimr; in the west, Vanaheimr (Vanir-world). In the middle, above Midhgardhr, is Ljossalfheimr (light-elf-world) and above that Ásgardhr, the enclosure of the Æsir, which houses many dwellings. Below Midhgardhr is Svartalfheimr ("black-elf-world "or "dwarf-world") and below that Hel, the silent, still, and sleepy realm of the dead. Between and among these worlds the runes and their roadways are to be found—here a great rune lies hidden.

Manifestation of the Rune Row

The manifestation of the runes and their ordering in the futhark row are bound up with the cosmogonic and cosmologic processes. The runes have no point of origin; they are the substance of the latent energy contained in Ginnungagap. The runes exist simultaneously in an undifferentiated state throughout this void—and thus defy comprehension. At the division between Muspellsheimr and Niflheimr, the runic forces are polarized into shining runes (ON *heidhrúnar*) and dark runes (ON *myrkrúnar*). These are polarized aspects of the entire corpus of runic power expressed simultaneously. These runic forces attract one another, in order that they might rejoin and create the cosmic seed of manifestation contained in Ymir. The shining runes and dark runes are re-assimilated in a pattern capable of manifestation. The runic forces are at work throughout the cosmogonic processes described above; however, the runes as we know them have not been manifested, because the entire process, up to the sacrifice of Ymir, takes place in an unmanifested state. When Ódhinn, Vili, and Vé sacrifice Ymir (the crystalized seed form of the collective runic pattern), they *arrange* this runic "substance" in accordance with the multiversal pattern. Thus they "create" the Nine Worlds and Yggdrasill. This primal act brings about cosmic order and manifestation.

At this point the runes are ordered in the futhark row in their linear form as the primary arrangement at the center of the multiverse. This manifestation unfolds from the "inside out," beginning with the most basic forms of cyclical (: ◊ :) and vertical (: ↑ :) force. From that point the other runes manifest themselves in a linear pattern governed by a twelve-fold spherical law. As each succeeding circle is manifested, a pair of runes—esoteric concepts—are isolated within the "space." The laws of sympathy and antipathy determine which runes crystalize in each circle. Also, those same laws govern which of these two concepts will be aligned with which previously manifested rune in the row. The row thus produced is perceived by the intellect in an order governed by the path of the sun, and thereby the runes manifest their numerical values 1 through 24. These numerical values are also part of the innate relative positions of one mystery to the others, and play a determining role in their ordering. A graphic representation shows the full glory of this mystery in Figure 3.1 on the following page.

These patterns, as well as those that govern the linear alignment of the staves, are fruitful avenues of meditation and will reveal much wisdom and provide great power to the vitki who can unravel their riddles.

Figure 3.1 represents only one of several patterns in which the runes are arranged or divided—each world or "realm of being" has its own particular modality. The ættir are ruled by the pattern of the eightfold "cross" or "star" by which the ancient Northmen divided the heavens (see Figure 3.2).

This rudimentary and fragmentary exposition of runic cosmology is only a hint of the secrets and splendors to be discovered by the vitki who perseveres, and penetrates the wisdom of the worlds.

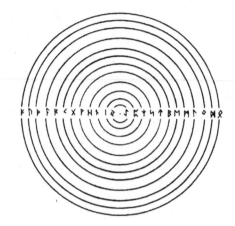

Figure 3.1 Diagram of the futhark pattern of manifestation.

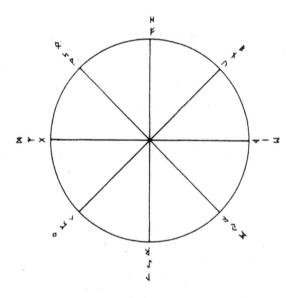

Figure 3.2 The eightfold division of the futhark.

Elements

Throughout the sections on cosmology we spoke of forces that *we* might call "elements," such as fire, water, ice, air, and earth. These are reminiscent of the Platonic-Hermetic elements of fire, air, earth, and water, but they are not to be understood as being identical with them. Both systems have common roots in the Indo-European spring of wisdom, which recognizes observation of nature (both internal and external) as the most reliable clue to the nature of numinous reality. The proximity of the Northern peoples to the realms of ice led them to recognize the multiversal dichotomy between fire and ice—which fits quite well with the message of modern physics. A short analysis of the attributes of these runic elements will help the aspiring vitki discover the interlace of these concepts with those of the rune staves, as shown in Table 3.1.

Table 3. 1. Attributes of Elements

Elements	Attributes
Fire	Total expansion, heat, all-vibration, archetypal energy
Air	All-pervasiveness and omnipresence, formless space, motion, light, intellect, communication
Water	Archetypal, unmanifested form, evolutionary being, stillness, darkness, unconscious
Ice	Total contraction, coldness (distinct from isa), no-vibration, cohesiveness
Earth	Total potential (containing all the others), archetypal manifestation and framework, physical matter, existence

An intuitive "feel" for these ideas will serve the vitki well in understanding cosmological mysteries, as well as providing emotional links to the various runes.

Streams

Much work has been done by German runic magicians concerning the intake and manipulation of streams of runic force. These streams may be classified according to the realms in which they originate: (1) terrestrial streams, which run along the surface of the earth; (2) heavenly streams, which circulate in the atmosphere; and (3) chthonic streams, which flow in the subterranean sphere. These streams or fields constantly interact upon one another causing changes and fluctuations in the intensity and form of the force found in each realm. All runes exist in all realms; they are, however, concentrated and intensified in power within the realms most sympathetic to the force they embody. Through the practices of stadhagaldr and meditation the vitki is able to draw these cosmic streams into his or her own personal runic sphere, there to be integrated (for increased personal power) or re-projected in order to cause changes in accordance with the will of the vitki. The practical section on stadhagaldr explains how to manipulate these streams in more detail. The word *stream* is perhaps a bit misleading. Actually, these runic forces may be *felt* as a variety of sensations within the psyche. Some are indeed similar to flowing streams of power; others are akin to waves, or whirlpools, or utter stillness. Each vitki should explore the "feel" of each rune on its own terms. Once contact has been made, it will be unmistakable.

The Soul and Personal Power Concepts

To fully discuss the depth of this topic would necessitate a study equal to that needed to outline fully the complexities of the runic cosmology. It is, however, important to understand the basics of the old Nordic soul-construct and personal power conceptions, for these play a prominent role in the theories of rune magic. It is in this world that the magic of the runes first arose, and the understanding—even the realization—of these conceptions will take us far into the power of the runes.

Certain soul qualities were given to the primal man and woman (coequally and simultaneously) by the triad of gods. This triad, which is a threefold expression of the god usually known as Ódhinn, was identified above as Ódhinn, Vili, and Vé. In another account, given in the "Völuspá" we read:

Until the Æsir,
mighty and loving,
came from the host
to the coast;
on the land they found
of little might
Askr and Embla
yet unfated.

They had not önd,
they had not ödhr,

neither lá nor læti
nor good litr;

Ódhinn gave önd
Hoenir gave ódhr,
Lödhurr gave lá
and good litr.

The last three gifts indicate external qualities (*lá*, appearance; *læti*, movement; *litr*, health), which are extremely important but not of central interest here. Önd is the breath of life, the "spirit" that is the "divine spark" in mankind and that all-pervasive force that penetrates and animates the multiverse. (This is very much akin to the Indian conception of *prana*, breath, and is etymologically connected to Sanskrit *atman*: soul.) Odhr is the power of inspiration and ecstasy. The name Ódhinn is derived from the same root word. This is that pure and irrational numinous power that is the magical faculty of gods and men.

With the entrance of the Nornic force, time and the laws of cause and effect arise (see the P-rune). Furthermore, the infusion of divine structure and consciousness provided by Heimdallr/Ódhinn (see M-rune) provides another numinous force, which is handed down through the generations. This force is increased or decreased according to human action throughout the life of an individual. These concepts are expressed throughout the rune row. With these qualities the development and concentration of magical power become possible—and even necessary.

Four principal entities arise from this complex interplay of runic forces and are centered in mankind: (1) *hugr*, (2) *hamr*, (3) *hamingja*, and (4) *fylja*. The hugr is the conscious will and intellect. The hamr is the personal aspect of the plastic image-forming essence in the cosmos. This is the realm of images, which bridges the worlds and acts as a matrix between the "spiritual" and "physical" worlds. A powerful hugr can project and even reform this personal essence in another location in an almost "physical" manner. The Norse sagas abound with accounts of this type. Most readers will be reminded of such phenomena as astral projection, and bilocation. The complex entity that gives this power is known as the hamingja, a term that means "shape-changing force," "luck," "power," and on occasion "guardian spirit." Hamingja may be transferred from one person to another, from a person to an object, or merely projected into space as indicated above. This force may be increased continuously by ritualized magical action and deeds of honor.

The fylgja is the storehouse of this action, which is symbolized by a female figure, an animal (specific to the internal nature of the individual), or a crescent shape that hovers before the person. Fylgja (fetch) constantly interacts with all levels of the personality imparting the ørlög or "fate" of the person in accordance with past action. Both the hamingja and fylgja may be passed from one generation to the next as a type of "reincarnation." The use of these qualities and entities in magical operations will be elucidated in some of the sections on practical work.

Basic Theories of Rune Magic

The forces used in magic and ritual may be divided roughly into two categories: the dynamistic and animistic. The dynamistic powers are more mechanistic, without a large degree of what *we* would call consciousness or will, other than their singular (or complex) functions. It is within this category that *we* may place the runes, and the multiverse generally. However, they do have a degree of "animism" about them, as personal investigation will show. The primal runic forces also are at the root of all being, as the section on cosmogony demonstrated. All the various wights, gods (Æsir and Vanir), elves, dwarves, and giants (thurses and etins) belong in the animistic category. The gods are archetypes, or exemplary models of consciousness, that are perceived as animate primordial images. These forces are ultimately derived from the dynamistic nature of the universe—as is mankind, which they help to form.

These exemplary models are also extremely useful in magic of course, either as internal consciousness factors or as symbols or vehicles for consciously directed power in invocatory rites. This latter type of rite is infrequent in common runecraft and belongs more to the magical religious expression of Ásatrú. In the old Nordic multiverse these two categories were closely interwoven. The following is a simplified model for the understanding of the runic processes at work in practical magic.

Regardless of what sort of power the magician works with, the main pattern of action is that of *communication*. The runes constitute a channel of connection between the will of the magician and the universe and its higher inhabitants who have the power to make things happen in this world.

There are also said to be rune streams present in the multiverse and they have their representative structures in the personal sphere in the hamingja of the vitki. This is similar to a macrocosmic-microcosmic model, except there is no definite boundary between the two. The "personal runes" and "world runes" are consciously synthesized in the magical/religious act according to willed or instinctual patterns. This is the essence of the Old Norse concepts *heill* (holy; wholeness) and *heill hugr* (whole mind), a high state of consciousness. The rune staves act as keys to give access to these streams in mankind and in the causal multiversal realms. As *symbols*, the rune staves (with the threefold nature) *are* the forces they "represent." Through willed ritual action the vitki is able to manipulate (through combination, Intensification, concentration, direction, etc.) the runic forces in the realms of the Nine Worlds. By the laws of perthro these actions become manifest as the altered rune streams react on and reverberate within 'the world in accordance with the will of the vitki. The efficiency of the vitki's work is in direct proportion to the intensity and quality of the impression he or she is able to bring to bear on the image worlds that are adjacent to Midhgardhr. The ancients knew that all "things" were filled with runic force—all things "had their runes." Rune wisdom is access to and knowledge of these modalities that penetrate and vivify all the worlds.

Although this book does not contain invocatory magic of a specifically "religious" nature, it is nevertheless important to understand the god-forms that are housed in the rune realms. These gods and goddesses are holy archetypes and consciousness modalities, that preexisted the self-consciousness of mankind but are intensified by human action. These images are culturally distinct exemplary models. They are to varying degrees self-conscious. For example, the rime-giants have practically no consciousness and are almost purely mechanistic, while the god Ódhinn is "structurally" as complex as the most complicated human being. These wights occupy various worlds, each according to their kind. There are, however, no well-defined borders between most of these realms.

For practical purposes and future reference, it would be well to explore the structure of the divine relationships in the worlds of the gods (Æsir and Vanir). The runic god-forms may be understood in a threefold matrix plus a fourth category. To a large degree this divine paradigm is reflected in the social structure of the ancient Germanic (and Indo-European) peoples. The mysteries of the M-rune explain this phenomenon.

The "divine society" is based on a tripartite system. The three levels, or functions, of this system are (1) sovereignty, (2) strength, and (3) production. The first and third functions are dual in structure. The first level contains both the judicial and the magical aspects of "kingship," while the third function encompasses the divine twins and the holy brother and sister. The major gods and goddesses of the Germanic pantheon are arranged according to this pattern:

1. The Judge-King (Týr) or the Priest-Magician (Ódhinn)

2. The Warrior (Thórr, in his oldest aspect)

3. The Providers (Freyja and Freyr, or Alcis)

A short study of these deities will show the complexity that is possible within this paradigm. In Norse theology Ódhinn has aspects in all three levels, true to his shamanistic nature of traversing all worlds. Týr is considered a god of war because the old ones considered war to be a type of judgment, according to past action and amount of honor/luck (hamingja) gathered by that action. Thórr is the warrior of the gods. As opposed to Ódhinn and Týr, he actually fights the battles. But he is also important to the farmers because through his atmospheric power he breaks open the clouds and brings forth the fertilizing rains. Freyja is rather similar to Ódhinn in that she has aspects in all three levels: she is the goddess of fertility and the teacher of the magical arts of *seidhr* to Ódhinn, and half of all warriors slain in battle go to her in the realm of Fólkvangr. (The other half goes to Ódhinn in Valhöll, or Valhalla, "the hall of those slain.")

The fourth realm is that of "deified" dynamistic forces or natural phenomena within the cultic sciences (belonging to the magical function). These would include the sun (Sunna; Sól), the moon (Máni), and fire, which is embodied in the runes kenaz, naudhiz, and dagaz, and other "elements" and forces.

In ritual work this classificatory system shows the efficiency of these deities in various types of operations. Gods and goddesses that belong to the third level are powerful aids in rites aimed at fertility, art, craft, wealth, and eroticism, while those of the second function rule in operations concerning protection, defense, liberation, and curses. The first level is rather all-encompassing, but the Týr aspect is most valuable in rites of law and order, justice, and success or victory. The Ódhinn aspect is the most comprehensive and is especially powerful in rites to obtain wisdom, numinous knowledge, personal power, and to bind or constrict enemies.

Ódhinn has an important lesson to teach all aspiring vitkar. Like Ódhinn, the vitki should search restlessly *all* the worlds, seeking wisdom and power, always willing to sacrifice of self to self, and constantly sharing that wisdom and power with others of like mind. To the true Odinist no path or door in the multiverse is blocked or closed.

CHAPTER 4

RUNE WORK

Through a combination of the runes and the vitki's personal will and ability, all things are possible; but in order to gain this power the vitki must develop the skills basic to all ritual work: concentration, visualization, breath and posture control, and the art of incantation. Many of these skills may be developed haphazardly over the course of practical work. The failures incurred by this method often discourage aspiring vitkar. The best course of action is one in which some time is devoted to exercises designed to develop the basic skills necessary to the successful performance of runagaldr. It has been noticed by several investigators that the runic power is often slow to develop in people (this may be due to the centuries of widespread neglect) but that when the force manifests itself in the vitki's life, it is all-pervasive in its potency, unshakable in its strength, and overpowering in the stimulation it produces. This may indeed be due to its innate or indigenous nature. A vitki of patience and perseverance will be well rewarded!

An elaborate and extensive set of exercises is presented in the book *The Nine Doors of Midgard*.

Foundations of Rune Magic

This book is not intended to provide the basics necessary to *all* forms of magic, but the following simple exercises can give some important clues to the nature of the developmental program that each vitki should design for himself or herself. Those who already have considerable experience in the magical arts may dispense with this stage and begin a program of practical experimentation if they desire. It must always be kept in mind that these basic skills should be constantly improved and practiced *daily*, because an increased intensity of will and concentration with more vivid visualizations will greatly expand the success of the magical operations performed by the runester.

Preliminary Exercises

I. Consult the runic commentaries and find a rune that is particularly appealing to you. Fashion a meditation card from a piece of white poster board about three inches by five inches in size. Paint the chosen stave on the card in bright red (enamel paint is good for this purpose). Sit in a comfortable position with the card in front of you at *eye level*. Begin an even breath rhythm, which should be maintained throughout the exercise. Spend some minutes concentrating on the form of the stave while silently chanting the name three times—pause—then again three times, continuing in this rhythm throughout. Keep all of these elements of concentration on shape, sound, breath, and posture under control for several minutes, then close your eyes and imagine the shape in your hugauga—your "mind's eye.". Continue practicing this until you can perform it smoothly for ten minutes.

II. Essentially, repeat the process of Exercise I, except sing the name (and basic galdr if you wish) out loud while maintaining a breath pattern of ten seconds inhalation—two seconds hold in—ten seconds exhalation (while singing the name or one line of the galdr)—and two seconds hold out. At this point begin experimenting with other simple postures, both sitting and standing. Always maintain the posture in a concentrated state, but *do not strain*. Again, concentrate on the card for some minutes, and then close your eyes and imagine its form blazing with vivid power. Once you can maintain this complex of action in a concentrated form for ten minutes, you may progress further.

III. Perform this exercise in the I-rune stadha with hands overhead. Set up a ten-two-ten-two (or as similar as is comfortable) breathing rhythm while facing north. With your eyes open or closed visualize first the F-rune in blazing red while intoning its name out loud three times. Slowly turn with the sun in a circle, visualizing and vibrating the form and name of each of the runes in turn while maintaining the stadha and breath rhythm. Once the aspiring vitki is able to perform this exercise in an almost instinctual fashion with few or no breaks in concentration, rune work may be confidently undertaken.

• • •

Besides a daily program of exercises of this type the vitki should design a course of intellectual and physical development in accordance with his or her will and intentions. The serious study of Norse mythology and religion and the science of runology, as well as the Old Norse language, will greatly improve the vitki's understanding of the processes of rune-craft. Because of the syncretic and "pantheistic" view of the multiverse contained in the runic system, a healthy, strong body will reflect itself in more powerful magical abilities. The true rune vitki is an awesome force on all levels of reality!

Magical Tools

The foregoing sections dealt with the "internal tools" of rune magic and their development, but the following pages are concerned with the "external tools" that symbolize internal forces. These are the traditional tools and techniques of runagaldr, which aid in the manipulation of the rune streams.

Attire

In the practice of runecraft the ceremonial vestments, while important, do not play a central role in the cultic symbolism. The magical attire of the vitki roughly corresponds to the everyday dress of an early medieval Northman, with special symbolic features. The main advantage of litur-gical vestments is the magical effect of setting oneself apart from every-day life that the donning and wearing of these garments should have. An ideal set of ritual attire for the rune vitki includes a hooded cloak or frock of a deep blue or black color as the outermost piece. Bright red pants also should be worn; this was a special sign of the vitki in ancient times. Black or natural-color heelless leather shoes may be worn, but many rites, especially those conducted outdoors should be performed barefoot. A pullover-type tunic of white, blue, or red should be worn under the cloak. This tunic should fit quite loosely and be girdled by a belt made of leather or deerskin. A sheath for the knife may be attached to the belt and a pouch may be hung from it to hold the various other magical instruments. The runes themselves may be represented in two places in the vitki's attire. A white headband may be fashioned, on which the runes are embroidered in bright red, and the wearing of a bracteate

Figure 4.1. A runic bracteate.

on which the futhark row and other magical symbols are engraved is a powerful aid in runic ritual. The bracteate should be made of bronze, gold, or silver. It should be designed, created, and consecrated in accordance with the vitki's level of skill and knowledge. An extremely basic design for practical purposes is shown in Figure 4.1.

Generally, male and female vitkar dress very much like; however, the female usually goes bare-legged or wears a long red skirt. Ritual nudity also is practiced, according to the nature and aim of the rite being performed. In this, as in all matters of magic, the vitki should let intuition be the primary guide.

Wand

The magic wand is known by many names in the technical language of Nordic magic; however, *gandr* is the most generic and expresses the powerful nature of this talismanic object. The gandr may be made from any of a variety of woods. The vitki might wish to consult Appendix D for some suggestions in this regard. In all cases the gandr should be cut, crafted, and consecrated according to the ceremonial formulas given for the rune tines below. The diameter of the wand should be no smaller than that of the index finger and no larger than the ring made by dosing the tips of the index finger and thumb. Its length may be as short as the length of the hand or as long as the distance from the fingertips to the elbow. The gandr is blunt or rounded on the hinder end while the forward end may be fairly pointed or moderately rounded. The vitki may carve all twenty-four runes of the Elder Futhark on the wand, arranged in the three rows of ættir—or, in accordance with knowledge, a more unique and perhaps more magically potent formula may be devised for this purpose. An example is shown in Figure 4 .2. Notice that the total number of runes is twenty-four, thus magically representing the entire futhark. The formula ek vitki is a potent magical statement that declares the power of the vitki and loads the object with his or her force. The numerical value of this part of the formula is 78 or 6 x 13 (see p. 106 for the section on numerical symbolism). The eight A-runes invoke the power of Ódhinn out of all eight corners of heaven.

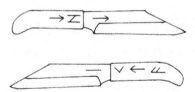

Figure 4.2. A runic wand. The inscription reads: ek vitki rist rúnar aaaaaaaa *(I the Magician carved the runes aaaaaaa.)*

Knife

The vitki's knife is often used to carve runes, but it is also employed to cut and prepare wood for talismanic purposes, or in rites of defense and invocation of runic forces. The hilt of the knife should be fashioned from wood or bone, and the blade should be of the "sax" type as illustrated in figure 4.3. Its total length is approximately nine inches with a blade five inches long and a width of about one inch. The name of the vitki, transliterated into runes (see Appendix B), may be etched into the hilt. Or a more complex formula may be devised to express the creative, shaping will of the runester. The illustration shows such a formula. It consists of three T-runes, which impart ordering successful force to the instrument, and a series of runes that ideographically express the nature of the knife. (| = the concentrated ego; ⟨ = controlled ability and creativity; ᚺ = the cosmic pattern it is intended to express; ᚠ = an invocation to Ódhinic force.) The numerical total of these seven runes is 81, which is 9 x 9—the intensified creative force in the multiverse. (See section on numerical symbolism).

Figure 4.3. A rune knife of the sax type.

Carver

A special carver is often used to etch runes into all types of surfaces. The *ristir* should be extremely pointed and sharp. It is often the most practical tool for the carving of runes. It may again bear the runic form of the vitki's name or a magical formula expressing the purpose of the ristir. A model for this is shown in figure 4.4. The inscription is *lathu futh:* "I (which means both the vitki *and* the ristir) invoke, or load, the futh." The final three-rune formula is the first three staves of the row, and represents the entire futhark. This formula may be called "the womb of the runes" (Old Norse *fudh* means vulva and vagina). The numerical analysis is 36, or 4 x 9 (see section on numerical symbolism).

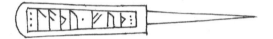

Figure 4.4. A rune carver (ristir).

Coloring Tools

The runes always were colored with either red pigments or blood. The magical significance of this is obvious. To the ancient Germanic peoples the verbal constructs "to make red" and "to endow with magical power" were synonymous. German *Zauber* (magic) and Old Norse *laufr* (magic, talisman) are both descended from this concept. In the technical terminology of ancient runecraft the Proto-Germanic word *fahido* and the Old Norse form *fa* meant literally "I color" and "to color," respectively. But these terms came to mean "to fashion runes" in general describing the entire complex process of carving; coloring, and consecrating the staves.

Pigments used by the old vitkar were red ocher, minium (red lead), and madder. Minium is a latecomer, but ocher was known from Neolithic times. Madder is obtained from the root of the plant of the same name *(rubia lincluria).* The Old Norse form of madder is *madhrn,* and the magical power of the plant is no doubt increased by the magico-affective association of this world with madhr, the Old Norse word for "man" (: ᛗ :). All of these pigments are available in some form at art supply stores. They should be ground with linseed oil, or a gum mixture, in a ritual manner just prior to the beginning of the runic rite. Linseed is, of course, derived from the seed of the flax plant, which is extremely important in runecraft. Its ancient name *lina* often appears in runic talismans for fertility, growth, and well-being. During the grinding process the futhark or the runes to be used in the rite should be intoned, infusing the dye with the potential energy of those runes. All of these pigments are symbolic substitutes for the innate magical power held by the blood, either human or that of a ritually sacrificed animal. If blood is used, no "preloading" is necessary. However, since the blood runes, the sanguine mysteries, are part of the religious expression, many vitkar will not concern themselves with them. *All* of the rituals in this book certainly may be performed powerfully using these venerable dyes.

A special tool should be made for inlaying the pigments into the carved staves. This can be made from a piece of wood about as thin as a veneer, which is cut in the shape of an isosceles triangle and inscribed with suitable runes. Figure 4.5 shows a *galdrastafr* made up of four K-runes, three in the form ᚲ and the connector in the alternate form ᚴ. Ideographically, this is an intensification of the kenaz-force. The numerical symbolism is also quite potent: 4 x 6, or 24 (a magical inten- sification of kenaz in the context of the whole futhark).

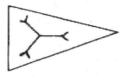

Figure 4.5. A runic coloring tool (reddener) bearing a powerful bind rune.

Magical Space

Rune magic may be performed indoors or out, but for atmospheric rea- sons, as well as for promotion of practical direct contact with the full power of the rune streams, outdoors is preferred. Ideally, the vitki would perform these sacred rites in a holy grove of oak, ash, or yew trees situ- ated high on a hill. However, any secluded place in a wooded area can suffice. The actual work space is conceived of as a sphere, and therefore a circular space should be cleared and ritually set apart in the manner outlined in the "opening ritual" on p. 97. Here we are concerned with the symbols to be contained in this magical space. The symbology may be as complex or as simple as the vitki desires; there is no dogma in this matter. Generally, when the work is done within an enclosed space, the symbolism tends to be more complex, and we would expect to find an altar, which may be either circular or rectangular, in either the northern or eastern sector of the space, or even in the center.

At this point a note on Germanic magical orientation should be interjected. From the earliest times the orientation was either to the east (as linguistic evidence shows) or to the north (as archeological evidence demonstrates). The English word *evening* ultimately derives from a Proto-Germanic root *aftan-*, which meant "backward"; hence, it indicates the observer faced eastward at twilight. There exists a large body of lore that speaks for a northward orientation. The Christian missionaries had problems compelling recently "converted" Germanic pagans to pray eastward instead of their heathen custom of facing north. The Icelandic *hof*, or temples, were lined up on a north-south axis, and even in the oldest period the passageways of the grave mounds faced northward. It is probable that both these directions were considered powerful and that each was used depending on the type of ritual involved—eastward for matters concerning the earth and northward for matters concerning the "other worlds." Most modern rune vitkar prefer north for the same reason those missionaries hated it.

The altar itself will contain all the objects necessary to the rite. It will also serve as the "workbench" on which the rune tines are carved. In a ritual performed outside, a rock or tree stump serve well, but a portable altar also may be constructed for such cases.

As for the circle that symbolically defines the sacred space, it may be as simple as a circle drawn on the ground with the wand, or it may be complex as a glyph drawn on the floor of a *vé* with chalk or other material. The magic circle should indicate the eight divisions of heaven, which are symbolic representations of the eight otherworlds of Norse cosmology, and the runes should be portrayed in the outer ring, as shown in Figure 4.6. Other figures or names may be added as the vitki sees fit.

Figure 4.6. A typical rune magic circle or ring.

Magical Time

The timing of runic rites also is very important, and while complex, it is not so rigid or complicated as that of traditions more influenced by zodiacal astrology. To fully explain these factors would require an independent study of no small magnitude and would unduly complicate the present work. The most important criteria considered by the rune vitki are (1) season, (2) moon phase, and (3) solar position (time of day). The most auspicious times are dawn, midday, evening, and midnight. For increase of power the waxing moon is desired, but for constriction of force its waning phase is used. The best general time for *any* undertaking is in the nights of the new moon or just after, or the full moon or just before. Again, intuition is the best and most powerful guide in these matters. It should be noted that time and space are considered aspects of one another and both are measured by the *mjötvidhr* (the measuring tree [Yggdrasill]).

Other Magical Tools

Several rites require further instruments, and while the minor ones will be introduced in the pertinent sections, these are a few that bear mention here.

The vitki should possess a drinking horn or cup from which mead is often drunk. The horn may be a natural one, properly prepared, or a horn-shape vessel of precious metal; a cup may be made of wood, earthen ware, gold, or silver. In any case, the runes ᛟ ᛗ ᚱ ᚠ ᚱ ᛁ ᛦ should be ritually inscribed on it in the talismanic manner. These runes are transcribed as *óhrœrir* and mean "the exciter of inspiration." This is the name of the divine mead of inspiration and of the vessel in which it is contained (see the A- and G-runes). The numerical and ideographic symbolism of this formula are powerful. The rune count is 7, and its total is 87, 3 x 29 (see section on numerical symbolism).

A brazier, or fire-pot (ON *glódhker*), also may be needed in some rites. It can be made of metal or earthenware. This fire represents the quickening power of Muspellsheimr. In addition, two pieces of cloth—one black, one white, both preferably of linen—should be on hand. A leather thong, symbolic of the containing, binding force in the multiverse is commonly used.

The equipment of the rune vitki is characterized by its mobility. All major tools needed for the performance of an act of rune work should be so well concealed that no one would even notice their presence.

Signing and Sending of Runes

The practice of making runic gestures or signs was well known in ancient times. The Norse *godhar* or priests would make the "sign of the hammer" (ON *hamarsmark*) ⅃ or ℛ over goblets before drinking. The rite of signing persons and objects with holy signs was established well before the coming of Christianity, and in fact they adopted this practice from the Indo-European tribes because they could not eradicate it.

A rune may be traced or drawn in the air in front of the vitki with the palm of the right hand, the right index finger, the right thumb, or the rune wand. Some of the staves may be signed with both hands in a smooth and aesthetic gesture.

Visualization is an important aspect of these *signingar.* The vitki should actually send, or project, the image of the stave from a sphere of brightness in the center of the body, along a shaft of red light to the point where the rune is intended to appear. Once the beam has reached this distance, the vitki traces the form of the stave from the substance of light. The color of the light may be red or some other symbolic hue (e.g., the color ascribed to the rune in Appendix D). A special rhythm of breath should be observed during this practice. Inhale as the arm is raised, concentrate on the intake of önd. On exhalation, send and sign the stave while singing the name and/or galdr of the rune, either mentally or out loud.

When the runes are invoked before the vitki, the force may either be reabsorbed into the personal sphere of the runester, infused into an object as an act of loading or "changing, "or it may be *sent* to do work elsewhere. This type of ritual work will be more fully treated in its own section below. It is being introduced here as a kind of exercise because it is good practice to use this procedure in daily work and because it is found in the ritual of talismanic loading. This is one of the most powerful techniques available to the vitki, but one that must be practiced and mastered with extremely strong concentration and visualization to be completely effective.

Rituals of Protection

A ritual should be devised by the vitki that serves to banish all forces detrimental to the work at hand and to prevent the return of those powers. These forces are not "evil," just disadvantageous to the operation. There are three good formulas for such a ritual. The hammer rite (*Hamarssetning*) is the strongest and provides maximal protection and isolation, the

Hagalaz rite provides the most potent magical atmosphere and potential, and the Elhaz rite strikes a balance between these. The formula outlined below gives the hammer rite, but to perform the other two simply substitute the word *hagalaz* or *elhaz* (elk) and sign the corresponding rune in the appropriate places. A rite of this type may be practiced every day and should be used in conjunction with an opening ritual to begin all ceremonial work.

The Hammer Rite

This example is written in a northward orientation, and appropriate changes of course should be made in the order of galdrar in rites of an eastward orientation.

1. With the rune wand in the right hand, face the North Star.

2. Beginning with fehu in the north sign and send the runes of the futhark in a ring around you at the level of the solar plexus as far out as the circle on the ground or floor, always "with the sun" in a clockwise direction. The runes should form a complete band ending with othala next to fehu in the north.

3. Stand in the cross stadha and visualize an equilateral cross lying horizontally in the plane of the rune ring and your solar plexus, with that point as the center of the cross. The arms of this cross should end at the points where they intersect the rune band. Imagine a surrounding sphere of shimmering blue light with the red rune band as its equator. Then visualize the vertical axis corning through your length from the infinite space above and from the infinite space below.

4. Feel and see the force flowing into your center from all six directions as it builds a sphere of glowing red might. The color may be altered depending on the ritual intention (see section on color symbolism).

5. The vitki should touch the hinder part of the wand to the breast at the center of power and thrust it forward, projecting the force from that center to a point on the inside face of the outer sphere. Then the runester should sign the hammer⊥ from the mass of magical might. The sign should be traced as in Figure 4.7 on page 96. During this process intone:

   Hamarr í Nordhri helga vé thetta ok hald vördh![3]
   (Hammer in the North hallow and hold this holy-stead![4]*)*

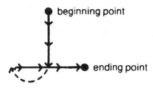
beginning point

ending point

Figure 4.7. Tracing pattern of the hammer sign.

Then, turning 90° to the right, send and sign another hammer sign vibrating.

Hamrr í Austri helga vé thetta ok hald vördh!
(Hammer in the East hallow and hold this holy-stead!)
Hamarr í Sudhri helga vé thetta ok hald vördh!
(Hammer in the South hallow and hold this holy-stead!)

And in the West:

Hamarr í Vestri helga vé thetta ok hald vördh!
(Hammer in the West hallow and hold this holy-stead!)

Returning to the north, direct your attention overhead, there send and sign the hamarsmark on the "ceiling" of the sphere, saying:

Hamarr undir mér helgn vé thetta ok hald vördh!
(Hammer over me hallow and hold this holy-stead!)

And then project the hammer sign below to the "floor" of the sphere (*not* the ground or room floor) and intone:

Hamarr undir mér helga vé thetta ok hald vördh!
(Hammer under me hallow and hold this holy stead!

6. Now, strike the cross stadha again and sing:

Hamarr helga vé thetta ok hald vördh!
(Hammer hallow and hold this holy-stead!)

Turning in the center of the *vé*, repeat this once for each of the other four directions and once for the vertical axis. The visual effect should be one of axes connecting all six shinning red hammers to your personal center, all engulfed by a field of sparkling deep blue light and surrounded by a band of bright red runes.

7. Finally, center all the forces of the *vé* by folding your arms from the cross stadha in toward your center, with your fingertips touching at the solar plexus, and saying:

Um mik ok í mér Ásgardhr ok Midhgardhr!
(Around me and in me Ásgardhr and Midhgardhr!)

This ritual may be repeated at the end of a working or exercise, and the entire sphere may be drawn into the personal center, or the walls of the globe may be split with the knife allowing the collected energy to flow to its goal.

The basic form of the rite given here is intended to shield the consciousness of the vitki for magical or meditational work. Modifications in the rite, such as the ones already suggested, may be worked out so that this ritual form may be used as an active magical tool. The runes on the face of the sphere may be drawn from, or projected through to, the outside in order to create magical effects. It is up to the runester to discover the further powers of the hammer rite lying beyond these instructions.

If a rune-worker is lucky enough to have a permanent sacred space then this working does not need to be repeated each time. The hammer rite outlined here is best seen as a way of making sacred space highly mobile.

The Opening Ritual

In important ritual work the vitki may wish to recite an invocatory galdr into which the hammer rite may be incorporated. Such a galdr would serve to invoke divine forces or simply act as a general invocation to the runic powers, or both. The knowledgeable vitki will compose his or her own rite and galdr, for this would be a great deed of runecraft! Note how the hammer rite is interwoven into this example:

1. Standing in the middle of the *vé*, face north or east, in the stadha and intone:

Fare now forth
mighty Fimbultýr[5]
from heavenly homes all eight
Sleipnir be saddled,
hither swiftly to ride:
Galdrsfadhir,[6] might to give and gain.
Holy rune-might flow
from the hooves of Hangatýr's[7] steed;
in streams of steadfast strength—
through slaves of stalwart standing!

2. Go to the northern (or eastern) rim of the *vé* and with the wand trace the circle in the direction of the sun. from left to right. During this process sing:

The rune-might is drawn
'round the holy-stead,
unwanted wights wend way!

3. When the circle is complete return to the center and facing the original direction, perform the rune-ring portion of the hammer rite. When this is complete say:

The worrisome wights now wend their way
eastward toward etin-home;
hallowed be the hall of Hroptatýr,[8]
with the help of Hrungnir's slayer![9]

4. Now perform the rest of the hammer rite.

5. After which, if the ritual calls for a brazier, the fire should be enkindled. If the vitki knows it, and the ritual needs it, this fire may be enkindled by the need-fire friction method; but normally, the runester will light the fire-pot with a previously prepared flame. Also necessary at this juncture are containers of salt and brewer's yeast; a pinch of each should be added to the flame at the point indicated in the galdr. Lighting the brazier, sing:

Endless light of life
give thy living gift
fill the night of need:
to the hearth of this hall
bring thy boon so bright
to quicken this salt
and yeast all so cold
together live long and well
in the hearts of Hár's[10] sib.

6. Once the fire-pot is enkindled, the vitki also may add leaves, thin strips of wood from trees, or herbs that correspond to the intention of the rite to be performed (see Appendix D). The body of the magical ritual may now begin in a "loaded" atmosphere.

The Closing Ritual

When a rite has been begun with an opening formula, a closing rite is in order.

1. Face north or east in the Ⴤ stadha and intone:

   Now is done the holy work of word and deed
   helpful to godly children
   hurtful to etin-churls
   hail to (him/ her/ them) who speak(s) them
   hail to (him/ her/ them) who grasp(s) them
   needful to (him/ her/ them) who know(s) them
   hail to (him/ her/ them) who heed(s) them.[11]

2. At this point the hammer rite (without the rune ring) may be performed, although this would be optional.

3. If it is not *totally safe* to allow the brazier to burn itself out, extinguish it by placing a cover over it with the words:

   Fire that glows without
   forever be kindled within
   by the might of Ódhinn-Vili-Vé.

4. If the energy built up by the entire operation is to be internalized, then draw the collected energies into your personal center by standing in the cross position, and while deeply inhaling, draw your arms in so that your fingertips touch your solar plexus. Turn in all four directions and repeat this action, each time visualizing the sphere being drawn into your center. If the energy of the rite has been sent abroad, then you may simply split the sphere with your hand or knife and step out of the circle.

Runic Meditation

The practice of both ceremonially and informally meditating on the runes is a source of vast wisdom—and a direct source of magical power. The vitki should strive to develop a personal link with each rune by communicating with the mystery on a deep level. Once this link has been made—with each individual rune and with the runic cosmology as a whole—a floodgate of runic force is opened, creating a stream of wisdom that always stands open to the vitki. Afterward this stream may be tapped even on an informal basis, in any spare moment that allows for reflection. Often these odd moments provide the vitki with some of the most powerful insights into the runic mysteries.

This meditation is an active, seeking endeavor. One of the most important techniques needed for success is the control of thought—that is, the submersion of thoughts detrimental to the purpose of the meditation and a guiding of the thoughts along the willed rune path. Once the hugr has been stilled and thought patterns have been concentrated into a single center—the rune—then the rune wisdom will begin to well up in the consciousness (hugr) of the vitki. The focal point of runic meditation is threefold: form (which may include color), sound (galdr) and root idea (contained in name and key words). The vitki should strive to concentrate, in a relaxed manner, on any one or all elements contained in this threefold complex, quietly leading detrimental thoughts out of the hugr and leaving only the runic symbols of form, sound, and name (root idea)—until finally the rune begins to speak directly to the consciousness of the vitki.

Ceremonial runic meditation may be as elaborate or as simple as the vitki desires or is able to perform. Generally, it seems that the wisest path is that which works from simplicity toward complexity. Preparations for meditation include the procurement of a quiet location, mastery of one of the protection-invocation rites, and the creation of a set of meditational cards, as described in the previous section. Later, mastery of the stadha of the chosen rune may be necessary. In the first stages of the meditational program the vitki may want to concentrate on one element of the threefold complex only, and include the others according to a self-directed program. A vitki should plan a progressive scheme that is suited to his or her own needs and abilities, always building a richer complex of elements in the inner center of concentration, while including a wider variety of magical techniques in the outer procedure.

The following is a composite outline of various methods of runic meditation from which the vitki may draw in the formation of a meditational program. All procedures may be physically performed, or if more convenient or effective, they may be performed totally within the hugauga.

1. Perform one of the protective-invocatory rites while strongly visualizing the rune ring.

2. Assume a comfortable position, either sitting or standing, or in the stadha of the proper rune. You may face either north, east, or in the angle indicated by the rune's position in the rune ring.

3. A runic meditation card should be set in such a position-attached to the wall or placed on a simple stand—that it is at eye level during this phase of the procedure.

4. With your eye fixed firmly on the runic form represented on the card, softly sing the rune galdr (this may be done inwardly). At the same time, if you wish, you may introduce formulaic *ideas*, such as the rune name, on a secondary level of consciousness. A name is of course included in the galdr; however, here we are considering the esoteric *meaning* embodied in the name, which may be included in the "center of concentration." In this phrase the vitki should strive toward a strong concentration on the elements of the runic complex that are intended.

5. The vitki should now slowly close his or her eyes, continuing with the galdr *a*nd contemplation of an esoteric principle (if included). Visualize the form of the rune as it appears on the card and in the mind's eye, and furthermore, attempt to realize the oneness of the form-sound-idea complex. In the beginning you may have to open your eyes to reestablish the stave form, but eventually you may eliminate the fourth phase and proceed directly to a complex inward contemplation once you are confident of your abilities.

6. Maintain this state of inner concentration on the runic complex for at least several seconds, preferably working toward a span of five minutes.

7. After this period of inward concentration the vitki should lapse into inner silence. But remember this is a totally attentive silence! During this void of slumbering thoughts, the word of the rune will be intoned with a resounding peal. This is a "word" that cannot be expressed by any language, but it is the totality of the runic mystery expressed in a single moment. This is a holy experience in which the rune and the hugr of the vitki are momentarily unified—or this unity is perceived.

8. The vitki may continue the meditation as long as a link with the runic force is felt. In this meditative state the vitki may be led along a myriad of rune paths, in which secrets concerning the rune itself

are revealed or the relationships between certain runes are made clear—the possibilities are infinite.

9. Once the linkage dissipates, or the vitki desires to terminate the meditation, simply repeat a formula such as "Now the work is wrought" and open your eyes. Then ritually break the rune ring according to the hammer rite.

After you feel yourself really becoming a part of the rune world, more informal meditational operations may be undertaken. These will reveal a vast amount of both usable and fascinating wisdom. It has been found that the most useful tools in this endeavor are paper, pen, compass, protractor, and perhaps even a calculator. The procedure is quite simple: Sit at your writing desk or table, surrounded with various runic glyphs and cosmological configurations. Still your mind, turning it toward the rune world. Allow your hugr to wander until it lights on a seed concept, then relentlessly follow it, drawing and jotting down your "revelations" as they come to you. These notations can then serve as the basis for further work—they will not often be candidates for the round file. It is probably best not to schedule these informal sessions but rather to sit down and delve into the mysteries when the "spirit moves you." Usually, after a short period of time the wisdom of the runes will begin to well up in the hugr of the vitki at odd moments. Sometimes the eruption of these forces is so powerful as to cause psychokinetic phenomena in the physical proximity of the vitki.

The regular practice of runic meditation is one of the mainstays in the overall rigging of rune wisdom and one that gives ample rewards for efforts well spent. It may be said that indeed the moments of inspiration gained from these practices are not akin to the discovery of a golden tomb in an exotic desert land but rather to the recovery of a long-lost family heirloom out of the attic (look in the basement too!). What has been lost can be regained if only the will is strong!

Talismanic Magic

In Old Norse there are three principal words for "talisman," "amulet," or "talismanic magic." They are (1) teinn, which indicates a piece of wood or twig fashioned into a talismanic object (the word "tine" reflects this); (2) hlutr, which may be any object used for talismanic or divinatory purposes (English "lot"); and (3) *taufr*, which means both talisman and magic in general; but in the original sense talismanic magic is particular. All three terms are quite descriptive of various aspects of talismanic runecraft.

The following section on taufr will deal with many features of rune magic, such as bind runes and the symbology of number, color, and ideograph, which are of vital importance in *all* areas of rúnagaldr but are introduced here because of the fundamental role they play in the art of taufr.

A tine is a living being that has an ørlög to live out, one that has been bestowed upon it by the vitki. The runester gives the "object" life and then magically provides it with ørlög through the nature of the runic power with which the vitki loads it. The "living nature" of the tine may be so strongly enforced that it will be found to have a "personality." In order to facilitate this high state of autonomous (but vitki-willed) force, the runester may wish to give the tine a name during the loading ritual. This is the mystery behind the many runic talismans (especially weapons) that have been given names.

The technical theories behind tine magic are in perfect accord with the laws of action within the runic cosmology in general. The rune tine acts as a key to unlock the power of particular rune streams. In the loading processes these streams (identical with hamingja) are willfully blended in the causal worlds and infused into the object, which has been prepared by the vitki with signs and staves receptive to those forces. There they are intensified or modified and again released, bearing a specific character imparted by the ørlög-giving galdrar and *formalár* of the vitki and the innate power of the symbols depicted on the tine. The talismanic form becomes linked to the essence of the particular rune(s) through a great concentration and energizing of forces directed by the vitki into the tine, using the shape, sound, and color of the runes.

Once the tine has been properly loaded, this power is then "unloaded" according to the form that the vitki impressed upon it. The object is the center of a vortex of force, receiving energy, formulating it in accordance with its ørlög, and then re-expressing it in the causal realms, leading to the desired result. This power also may be retained within the personal sphere. The efficiency of this process is dependent on the level of strength in the vitki's hamingja and the quality of concentration and visualization the vitki may bring to bear in the loading operation.

Another important aspect of tine magic is that of magical linkage to the "object" of the taufr, that is, the person or thing to be affected by the magical force. This may be brought about by attaching a runic formula to the object that represents the person (such as the name transliterated into runes) or by the physical proximity of the tine to the person to be affected. Other techniques of sympathetic magic also may be employed.

There are several distinct types of runic talismans. Usually, they are fashioned from pieces of wood, bone, stone, or metal that readily take their forms. However, paper or parchment also may be used by those less traditionally inclined. The objects on which the runes and signs are carved may be purely magical in function or they may also serve some utilitarian function. The former group is what is usually considered a tine. The latter group may include such objects as belt buckles, pens, automobiles, screwdrivers, guns, and so on, that are thus endowed with hamingia. This is valuable for imparting success or protection in the areas where the object is used. This tradition is just as useful and powerful today as it was in ancient Europe, when warriors inscribed their weapons and shields with runes for protection and victory. The imagination of the modern runester should prove to be a fruitful guide in this practice. Another class of talisman is stationary. Any fixed object may be turned into a runic talisman. Trees, large rocks, and houses are good examples. Also, a stationary taufr may be a card or stave placed in the vitki's room, or a tine placed near the person to be affected by the magical force. These are used to influence magically a particular place to persons who are regularly in that place. The internally applied talisman is also known and will be discussed below.

The techniques of tine magic may be used in operations of every type. The procedures outlined in these sections should be followed, in one form or another, when fashioning tools to be used in the runic art.

Bind Runes

Tines may be produced that express a single runic force, but one of the most potent techniques of blending several runic forces together for a very specific purpose is that of the bind rune (ON *bandrún*). A bind rune is the combination of individual runic powers into one mighty field of action. This method has the distinct advantage for the modern vitki of using only the ideographic essence of the rune; therefore, the contemporary runester does not have to worry about whether his or her inscription is correct or whether it will be effective if written in Modern English. In order to properly build and load such a form, the vitki must have a deep understanding of separate runes and how they fit together to form a single powerful expression of force with a single harmonious will. The principles of spiritual and physical aesthetics are important here. This combining aspect is common to all runecraft, but with the bind runes it finds its most obvious expression.

Bind runes have been used by runesters from the very beginning. There are two main types of these bandrúnar: (1) those used to connect two or more runes together when inscribing words, and (2) those of an apparently purely ideographic type (although this last type may contain a word concealed in its form as a kind of simultaneous anagram). A great amount of "artistic license" is available to the vitki in the construction of bind runes. The alternate forms of the various staves should help in the formation of an aesthetically pleasing shape. When formulating bind runes, the runester always should keep the elements of numerological symbolism and ideological harmony and cooperation in mind.

When used in writing, bind runes may connect two runes or a group of them. This is done to form a magical link between these two runes, to represent two or more words in a coded form, or to reduce the overall count of runes in the inscription. A bind rune always is counted as one rune in the rune count (see section on numerical symbolism). The common grammatical ending -*az (-aR)* is often written ᚴ (note the use of an alternate form of the Z-rune to obtain the magico-aesthetic effect). Magically, this links the forces of the A and Z-runes into a special expression—which is quite powerful! One of the oldest bind runes is ᚷ , which represents ✕ plus ᚠ This stands for the magical formula *gibu auja* (give good luck) and is often carved on talismanic or ritual weapons. Any runes having adjacent vertical staves are prime candidates for binding, as are words (especially pronouns and verb forms) that are common, for example, ᛗ (*em*: I am); ᛗ (*ek*: I).

The purely ideographic bind runes are the most useful in tine magic, and their multiplicity of levels makes them very effective in refined operations of magic. One of the oldest examples of this is found on the brooch of Soest, c. 600–650 CE (see Figure 48). This is formed from the runes ᛉ, ᛁ, ᛏ, ✕, and ᚠ twice. The numerical total of these runes is 66, or 6 x 11, with a rune count of 6 (see section on numerical symbolism pp. 106–108). This galdrastafr is a love talisman carved on a brooch and then given to a woman. The power of the taufr draws upon Ódhinic force ᚠᚠ with justice and a call for success ᛏ, out of need ᛁ (note also the sexual symbolism here), for marriage (erotic union) ✕, according to ancestral principles and territory ᛉ. The rune count and multiple of 6 emphasizes the erotic nature of the talisman. The runes also may contain an anagram of the old German man's name *Attano* plus the sign X (marriage). The analysis of old inscriptions gives many clues to modern practice.

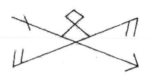

Figure 4.8. Bind rune found on the brooch of Soest, c. 600–650 CE.

Another ideographic example would be the "Three-headed *thurs*" (Figure 4.9). Essentially a threefold intensification of the THrune, this is used in curses. Further examples of bind runes will be given in the magical formulas.

Figure 4.9. Ideographic "three-headed thurs."

Numerical Symbolism

Numerical criteria play an important role in the loading and working of rune tines, and they are often critical in other types of rune magic. In the ancient inscriptions we sometimes find that the vitki has in some way sacrificed linguistic clarity for numerical (or ideographic) potency. This is done by leaving out staves (especially vowels), or by adding or doubling them.

As noted at the beginning of this book, *number* is one of the three keys to each rune. The commentary given under each rune is also pertinent to the symbolism of its number. Indeed, much of the interpretation is drawn from numerical criteria. Strong examples of this would be the H-rune (9)-the Nine Worlds of Yggdrasill; and the J-rune (12)—the twelve months of the solar year. It is necessary only to give the broad outlines of runic numerology here; the true vitki will find the right roads to further power.

The numerical values of inscriptions, tines, and magical formulas place the power of the runes in various "spheres of working" and also draw on the power inherent in that number for their working. Often it is best to aim for a harmonious and broad-based sphere of working to lend maximal overall power to the ideographic and linguistic form of the formula. These formulas also may modify or adjust the overall power of the whole. Since every formula and tine works on various levels simultaneously, a general rule of thumb would be the more levels of meaning you can pack into the least amount of space, and the more cryptic you can make it, the more effective the magic will be. This is important in the shaping as well as the interpretation of talismans.

Runic number formulas are analyzed in two ways: (1) the rune count, that is, the number of staves in the formula; and (2) the total of the numerical values of each rune in the formula (as in gematria). These numbers are then broken down into their multiples in order to further analyze their powers. A simple example of this process is shown in Figure 4.10: Rune count 8 (multiple: 2 x 4); runic total: 66; (multiple: 6 x 11). This formula is found on ancient talismans, and forms an incantation of great ideographic, phonetic, and numerological power.

ᛚᚢᚹᚨᛏᚢᚹᚨ

Figure 4.10. Runic number formula "luwatuwa"

Either or both of these systems may be used. The meaning of these numbers is twofold. They indicate the sphere in which the formula is to work and the power by which it works.

There are several "numbers of power" in both of these systems on which the beginning vitki could concentrate. For the rune count, the numbers 1 through 24 are all powerful, and imbue the formula with the force of the rune of that number. Also, the use of any twenty-four runes in an inscription provides a broad base of power and invokes the *force* of the whole rune row into the formula. To a twenty-four-fold rune count, the number eight and its multiples (and indeed twenty-four and its multiples) may be added to maintain the whole harmony of power while intensifying its force. The multiple of the rune count also modifies the runic potency in subtle and ingenious ways. These are common patterns in ancient inscriptions. On the second level, that of the numerical total of the runes, there are many possibilities and numbers of power, which direct the runic force in specific directions and give them special magical characteristics. Of course, the sums 1 through 24 indicate the sphere where that particular rune is at work. Prime numbers are especially powerful and express a tremendous amount of will. Whatever the runic total might be, it is through its multiple factors that the root force of the number is revealed. Multiples of three, and especially of nine, are powerful in operations dealing with magical forces working on many levels at once, including the earthly realm. Multiples of ten are especially forceful when the intent is to cause a change in the manifest world of Midhgardhr. Twelve and its multiples also are potent in this regard but have a more prolonged and enduring effect. The number thirteen and its multiples are the most universal numbers of power. A vast number of runic inscriptions manifest this numerological pattern. The number is indicative of universal potency and contains the mystery of eihwaz as the world-tree (9) and the three realms (3) in the ontological oneness of Ginnungagap (1). The number by which the "master number" is multiplied further modifies and directs the overall force of the formula according to its runic nature.

All of these principles may be used when constructing rune tines and rituals; however, they need not dominate the form of the operation. Let intuition and natural inclination be your guide. Vitkar may totally dispense with numerical considerations, and their results will in no way diminish. The correct use of runic numerology is an art in itself and one that needs to be supplemented with a large dose of Nordic lore to be completely effective. The study and analysis of inscriptions fashioned by our forebears should be the guiding light in our efforts. It also should be pointed out that the old Germanic attitude toward the concept of number was quite different from that held by their neighbors to the south. To the Pythagorean and Gnostic mystics, number came to be the ἀρχή (rule) of all things, but to the vitkar, number was only one among three equal expressions of the same holy mystery embodied by a rune. While the Gnostics and Pythagoreans tended to look at number as a way of measuring and distinguishing one thing from another, the vitkar saw them as points of connection and interrelation in a cosmos forever in a state of ebb and flow.

Color Symbolism

The symbology of color in the runic system is somewhat different from that of the Judeo-Christian culture, although the ancient Germanic traditions (among many others) have influenced the Christian color symbology to a certain extent. The source of this color system is to be found in the Eddas and in the saga literature. In the practice of runecraft this color lore is valuable as material in formulating powerful visualizations and ritual intensification as well as in the construction of more complex talismans. (See Table 4.1.)

Appendix D provides speculative color correspondences for each rune, but the best guide is the intuition of the independent vitki. In this manner, as in most others, the perspective of the consciousness alters the perception of the concept, and it is the perception that provides the *best* key for unlocking the concept.

Table 4.1. Color Symbology

Color	Interpretations
Gold	The light of the sun and the spiritual light shining from Ásgardhr, the force of önd in the universe and a symbol of honor, reputation, and power in all realms.
Red	Magical might and main, protective power, spiritual life and vigor, aggressive force. The principal color of the runes; also a sign of death. Often related to gold.
Blue	The all-encompassing, all-penetrating, and omnipresent mystical force of the numen, a sign of restless motion, the color of Ódhinn's cloak. In its darkest hues it becomes one with black.
Green	Organic life, the manifested force of fertility in the earth and in the sea, a sign of the earth and nature, passage between worlds.
Yellow	Earthly power, a sign of desire and lust in a will toward manifestation. Related to both green and gold.
White	The total expression of light as the sum of all colors- totality, purity, perfection, nobility, the disk of the sun.
Silver	The disk of the moon, change, transmutation, striving for higher knowledge. A metallic version of white.
Black	New beginning (as night and winter herald the birth of day and summer), all-potential, the root force of all things, knowledge of hidden things, concealment the container of light.

Pictographic Symbolism

Many runestones and rune tines also bear pictographic representations of holy concepts that aid in the formulation and direction of magical power. These are of two kinds: (1) pictographs, graphic representations of naturally occurring objects (see Table 4.2 for examples); and (2) ideographs, the holy signs or *galdrastafir* of rune magic (see Table 4.3 for examples). These signs and symbols work in conjunction with the runic forces, or they are embodiments of the force expressed by the rest of the formula. They are valuable as talismanic symbols and also as objects of meditation and material for magical visualization.

This short analysis should give the aspiring vitki a good basis for practical experiment, while the more curious vitkar will search out books on Norse symbolism and rock carvings for even more of these enchanting signs.

Table 4 .2. Pictographs

Symbol	Interpretation
	Serpent or Lingworm—enclosure, containment, chthonic force and the magical unconscious.
	Man and horse—wisdom and magical power of projection, swiftness, command over the worlds and spiritual realms, the Ódhinic force.
	Ship—passage between life and death, transmutation, fertility, and growth (often appears with ⊕ above it).
	Horn or caldron—sign of Ódhrœrir, wisdom and inspiration, invocation of eloquence.
	Hammer—Mjöllnir, the Hammer of Thórr, protection, increase, raw power, and will.
	Bird (raven)—swift-moving intelligence and memory.
	Moon—transmutation, ordered change, magical power.

Table 4.3. Ideographs

Symbol	Interpretation
⊥	Hammer—same as pictograph.
卐	Sunwheel or hammer—similar to ⊥, but also luck, solar power, the sign of the dynamic solar wheel, transmutation, and magical power underwill.
⊕	Solar wheel-spiritual power, law, order, contained religious force, holiness.
✳	Hagall/World-Tree—cosmic pat tern of Yggdrasill, the snowflake, protection and magical working by and through the laws of the world.
⊛	*Glückstern* (Star of Luck)—same as Hagall above. Common in Dutch hex signs and a powerful framework for talismans and visual magic.
✱	Heavenly star or cross—the eight corners of heaven, the eight legs of Sleipnir, the world-tree and the heavens expressed in a single ninefold pattern (center: Midhgardhr, the world of man).
⧉	*Valknutr* (the knot of the fallen, or chosen)—the Nine Worlds embodied in the three realms in eternal unity expressing the evolutionary law of arising-being/becoming-passing-away to new beginning.
⅄	Trefot—dynamic power from the three realms of being and the threefold evolutionary force. Made from three L-runes (21 + 21 + 21 = 63, or 7 x 9); magical inspiration throughout the cosmos.
♡	"Heart" (actually an ancient representation of female genitalia and buttocks)—sensuality, eroticism, love. In Old Norse books of magic the sign ⋈ often appears in spells of love magic; a symbol of sexual intercourse.

Talismanic Construction

Before attempting to construct a runic talisman the vitki should be well versed in the intellectual content of the rune lore and suitably advanced in the psychic faculties necessary to the successful completion of a talismanic operation. Rune tines should be constructed in accordance with the theories and ideology expressed by the runic system to be of maximal effect.

If the tine is to be constructed of wood, it should be fashioned from a kind of wood that is sympathetic to the aim of the talisman. For this the vitki may consult Appendix D, or better yet, let informed intuition be your guide. The possibilities of using wood are limitless. Metal disks, plates, or rings of copper, bronze, silver, or gold also make excellent runic talismans. Other materials, such as a small and appropriately shaped stone or piece of bone, also are favored. Larger stones are also good for stationary talismans, and in such cases the vitki will find it useful to have a hammer and chisel dedicated to the runic arts with which to construct these runestones. Earthenware is also receptive to rune loading; runes may be etched into the finished product or they may be cut into the soft unfired object, colored properly, and then fired—all in a ritualistic process with powerful potential. Runic talismans also can be formed from parchment colored with pens, inks, and paints dedicated to ritual practice. These parchment talismans may then be carried (in lockets, for example), or they may serve as stationary symbols. The imagination of the vitki is the only limit to the possibilities.

There are certain shapes that are best suited to receive runic forms. The most common are the rectangular solid, the thin wooden stave (1/16 to 1/8-inch-thick), the thin disk or rectangular plate, a segment of natural tree branch, or a cylindrical shape of various lengths. Pieces of jewelry of all types are prime candidates for talismanic use. A unique shape that is fairly common for talismans is a thin rhomboid. This is usually cut from wood or bone. Figure 4.11 shows a typical example of this type. By using this design, the vitki has four smooth surfaces available for longer inscriptions. This is also an extremely convenient and comfortable shape for tines designed to be carried on the person.

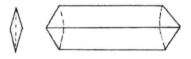

Figure 4.11. A typical talismanic (rhomboid) form.

Necessity will guide the vitki in the construction of utilitarian talismans. The main requirement in the external formation of these holy objects is that they contain a symbol or symbols describing the purpose and aims of the talisman and a "signature" representing the person, persons, or thing to be affected or altered by the force of the first symbol. This signature may indeed be the name of the person or it may be some other sympathetic link; even physical proximity may serve to form this linkage. Space on the object should be aesthetically allocated and divided according to rune staves, holy signs, and the signature. Any combination of these elements is of course acceptable. Figure 4.12 shows an example of a tine for increasing inspiration, magical power, and general success for a person named Erik Thurman.

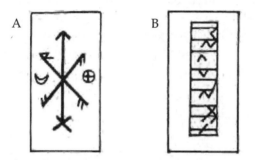

Figure 4.12. Bind rune talisman with signature. A) Obverse. A bind rune formed from ↑, ᚠ (twice), ᚠ, ᚱ, and ✕ providing success and energy in the realms of inspiration and magic in the natural order of things. B) Reverse. Note that certain runes are bound so that the rune count totals 7, thus linking the name with the power of magical inspiration.

The vitki should experiment with various surfaces and tools to determine what the best cutting techniques are for each. Time spent in the practice of carving runes will be well invested, because the more skilled the runester becomes in these basic mechanical skills, the more energy and concentration he or she can divert to the work at hand. One general technique that works well for all types of materials, is the precutting of rune bands; that is, cutting two grooves to act as upper and lower limits for the staves.

Cutting Wood for Rune Tines

Once a design has been decided on, the vitki should explore the neighborhood for the right tree from which to cut the tine. After this scouting process is complete, go to the tree in a ritualized attitude, armed with the rune knife, at a time that seems auspicious for the aim of the operation. Generally, the most favorable times are considered to be dawn, noon, and twilight. Find a branch or twig that bends toward a quarter or eighth (of the heavens), because that is sympathetic to the purpose of the tine. The choice of a root a t the time of midnight is effective for negative rituals and curses.

The cutting of the tine should be carried out in a ceremonial manner. First, standing to the north or east of the trunk, facing outward, perform the Hamarssetning or other suitable rite, envisioning the *whole* tree encompassed within the holy-stead. Then position yourself before the branch, twig, or root that you intend to cut. You may have to climb the tree to do this, of course. Turn your attention to the might and the wight of the tree with the words:

> *Hail to thee, might of (tree name)!*
> *I bid thee give this branch!*
> *Into it send thy speed,*
> *to it bind the might of the bright runes_____*
> *(names of the runes to be used)!*

Now proceed to cut the portion of the branch desired, while humming or singing the names and/or galdrar of the proper runes during the whole procedure.

Once the future talisman has been removed, the vitki should give thanks to the wight of the tree for its gracious gift.

> *Wight of (tree name), take my thanks*
> *henceforth be thy might in this branch!*
> *Deeply bound to the bright (appropriate rune names)*
> *working my will with speed.*

The branch may then be trimmed and prepared for receiving the stave forms. The tine may be ritually loaded in that place at once, or it may be saved until later and loaded in the runester's usual *vé.*

This ritual process may be adapted easily for the selection and preparation of other materials to be fashioned into holy objects by the runic art.

Ritual of Loading a Rune Tine

The following ritual description provides an example of the complete loading process from which the vitki will be able to devise similar operations for all types of runic talismans. The techniques outlined here are valuable in all kinds of rune work.

This taufr is built on the runic formula LAUKAZ, which appears very often on ancient bracteate talismans. Literally, the word means "leek" *(allium porrum)*, which is a symbol of growth and well-being. This is a lso an alternate name for the L-rune. The Proto-IndoEuropean root word from which the Germanic *laukaz* is derived is **leug-* (to bend, turn, wind), a powerful concept and one common to words having to do with magic. This formula promotes healthy growth in the field of things hidden and secret (the root word is also the ancestor of our word *lock*).

The numerical analysis of this formula reveals one of its many power sources. Figure 4.13 shows the rune count as 6 (multiple: 2 x 3). The rune total is 52 (multiple: 4 x 13). The number 6 indicates its working in the sphere of will-controlled magical arts (a doubling of the dynamic action of 3). The formula works from a magical (4: ᚠ) intensification of the vertical force of the numen (13: ᛁ) throughout the year of 52 weeks. The ideographic analysis is equally revealing:

1. ᛚ life-law / growth

2. ᚠ transformational numinous force

3. ᚢ unconscious wisdom, health

4. ᚲ conscious knowledge, ability

5. ᚠ transformational numinous force

6. ᛉ protection / "higher" life

The complementary conceptual relationships between the first and last runes, and the third and fourth runes, loaded with the magical "spirit" of the second and fifth runes (which are adjacent to all the others) show the ideological potency and scope of this formula.

ᛚᚠᚢᚲᚠᛉ

Figure 4.13. The LAUKAZ formula.

For the performance of this rite, the vitki will need a suitable setting for the ve with an altar of some type, the gandr, the knife or carver, suitably prepared blood or red pigment (and equipment for preparing this on site), the coloring tool, a black cloth (preferably of linen) large enough to enclose the tine, a leather thong or organic twine long enough to encircle the object nine times, and whatever ritual attire the vitki deems necessary. For optional phases of the rite the vitki also will need a brazier (and kindling) and a cup of water or mead. The talismanic object itself should be fashioned from a piece of willow wood (or its complement alder wood) having two flat surfaces of suitable size to take the inscriptions. This object should be fully dressed and prepared in its final form and shape except for the magical staves and signs.

Go to the site of the vé in silence, preferably at the hour of dawn. Arrange the implements in an orderly fashion on the altar and let the ritual begin.

1. Opening. Facing north, perform the opening rite including the ritual kindling of the brazier if necessary and Hamarssettning or other suitable opening formula. This invokes the rune might and calls upon the gods and goddesses as witnesses, while banishing detrimental forces.

2. Preparation of dye (optional). If the blood or pigment has not already been prepared, the vitki may grind it on location. If this is done, sit facing the altar, and grind the pigments with the galdr:

   laukaz la ukaz laikaz.
   [followed by the individual galdrar
   of all six runes in turn]
   Blood of Kvasir[12]
   be blessed:
   rune-might blooms in the blend!

3. Name carving. This is to provide the magical link between the power of the formula and the person to benefit from it. Turn the tine so that what is to be on the reverse side is facing up. Using the knife or carver, etch the runes of the person's transliterated name (see Appendix B) into the surface, using any formulaic devices that might help integrate the name (and person) with the power of the runic formula. Color the name with the pigments and recite a galdr such as:

Together the bright runes
are bound and blended
with the might of (name)!

This does not require a level of intense loading as high as that for the taufr formula. (This step is optional if the tine is to be worn on the person at all times.)

4. Preliminary galdr. Standing before the altar, gandr in hand, invoke the forces ᚱ ᚠ ᚾ ᚲ ᚠ ᛉ by thrice intoning the names of each in turn over the tine, and at the same time signing the stave shape over the object with each repetition of the name. This serves to make the material receptive to the streams of these runes.

5. Carving. Sit before the altar in a manner that has been taught to the vitki by personal experimentation. Carve each of the stave forms while singing the simple sound formula of the rune being etched. For continuants (sounds that can be produced as long as the breath lasts) the pure sound is best. In this inscription they are *l, a, u,* and *z.* The *k* sound must be coupled with a vowel and repeatedly intoned (*ka-ka-ka* . . .). During this process *feel, see,* and *concentrate on* the shining rune might as willfully flows from the heavens, earth, and subterranean realms via your center, through your arm and carving tool, into the wood in the shape of the stave. The opening ritual engaged these three realms for this purpose. The material on stadhagaldr and rune streams is also helpful in mastering this practice. Visualize the shining "substance" in white, red, or electric blue as it is inlaid into the grooves cut by the rune carver or knife. When each has been carefully carved in this manner, the vitki may wish to cut a straight line across the bottom of the staves, connecting their shapes to bind them together in a single form and field of force (in the case of this inscription the K-rune hovers, unconnected).

6. Coloring. Take up the container of paint or blood, and using the knife point or coloring tool, inlay the staves (and connecting bar) with the vivifying substance. This should be done with care and concentration. Throughout this process repeatedly sing the complete runic formula, *lllllaaaauukaaazzz* . . . . This imparts basic life force to the tine. At this point the vitki may wish to pause and concentrate on the power of the runes being loaded into the *form*—feeling their presence, as they vibrate with the substance of the wood, in the

consciousness of the vitki. Once this is completed, the runester may lightly rub a small amount of linseed oil over the surface of the tine. This serves both an aesthetic and a magical purpose.

7. Enclosure. This is the "dwelling in darkness" before birth and emphasizes the cyclical nature of the runic mysteries. The tine gathers and intensifies its strength during this separation from light. Take up the tine and wrap it in the black cloth, then bind it nine times around with the thong. During this process intone the following galdr, or one of your own composition containing similar concepts.

Into the den
of darkness deep wend thy way
—undoomed yet—
nights all nine
wile away thy spell.
Sleep, gain and grow
in weal and wealth.

Lay the tine down on the middle point of the *vé* and make nine turns (circumambulations) with the sun, while singing the complete word formula: *llllaaaauuukaaauz*. Return the object to the altar.

8. Birth of the living taufr. Unbind the thong and open the cloth while intoning the verse:

Hail thee day!
Hail day's sons
thou art born
—undoomed yet—
bearing my will
wend thy way
toward day's light
with life's law.

Now the vitki should bring his or her mouth close to the tine, and with maximal force of breath intone the holy formula *fffffaaaaaa . . .* , while feeling and visualizing a great outrush of hamingja into the creature. This also infuses the tine with intensified önd. In order to awaken the now indwelling wight, take up the gandr and gently knock thrice upon the form.

9. Naming (optional). If the vitki wishes to intensify the animate aspect of the tine, it should be ritually endowed with a name. This name should reflect the purpose of the talisman, and it is usually feminine in form. A good name for this tine might be Grœdhing(a) (growth, or the growing one). Pass the tine three times over the firepot intoning a verse indicative of the life-giving force, such as:

Now sparks of fire
with speed spew forth;
lend thy quickness and life.

Then lay the tine on the altar. Dip your fingers into the cup and carefully sprinkle the tine with the water or mead, with the formula:

I sprinkle thee with water
and give thee the name (name).[13]

10. *Formáli.* Now the tine wight must be permanently encoded with its special purpose—its "doom" or ørlög. It is newborn but must be provided with "past action," that it may more mightily fulfill its function. This is done by means of a formáli, or formal speech of declaration. Stand in the Ý stadha before the tine lying on the altar and proclaim a formula that outlines all the requirements, restrictions, and purposes of the talismanic being. For this tine, the following is appropriate:

Thou art wight of my will,
and 'tis thy doom to do as here is deemed:
Thou shalt shield my way,
wherever I may wend,
and with Asa [14]*—might and main,*
shower upon me
thy shining law of life
with a love of lust and shaping wisdom,
that I may grow and gain—whole and hale keep me—
as thou art young the whole year through.
In the name of Ódhinn-Vili-Vé
and by the might of Urdhr-Verdhandi-Skuld so
shall it be.

11. Holding. To bind the might of the rune load to the tine, trace three rings around the wight with the gandr while singing:

Rune-might hold
the holy runes;
whole may they
work my will.

Visualize a containing semipermeable sphere of shining force around the tine that allows the desired power to enter and be transformed, intensified, and re-projected but holds the original loading and prevents discharge by contrary forces.

12. Closing. After placing the tine in its intended bode, the vitki may sing a short closing verse:

Now the work
has been wrought
with the might
of mighty runes
so shall it be.

Or perform the closing ritual outlined above.

Now the living hlutr is to be placed where it is to live its life and perform its function. If the tine is to be worn on the person, it should be next to the skin suspended by a cord, thong, or chain made of sympathetic material.

Further Talismanic Formulas

The more advanced runesters will need no further clues to the successful practice of tine magic, but for those aspiring and talented vitkar who might need more clues, the following ritual and inscription formulas should be of some help. The first three introduce ancient and in some cases rather unique ritual methods that will be of special interest to all vitkar as yet unversed in the hoary and magical literatures of the sagas and Eddas. In the latter section, five talismanic formulas are provided for various magical operations. Some of these are drawn from ancient rune lore, while others are formulas created in the twentieth century. Here again it must be stressed that the most effective rituals will be those designed by talented vitkar based on their own personal relationship to the rune world.

The three special ritual formulas or patterns introduced in the following sections concern three of the most basic drives in magic: (1) love, (2) revenge (curse), and (3) wisdom. The main purpose behind the inclusion of these formulas is to *suggest* paths to greater runic power through a variety of techniques within the general realm of talismanic magic.

Love

Rituals to gain the love of another have been one of the principal subjects of runecraft since ancient times. However, as a previous example has shown, the successful attempts of runic love magic were performed with what we might today call "good intentions." This does not stem from any moralistic accretion in the runic system but rather from the complex nature of sexual energies and relationships. It simply seems that love magic *works* much more effectively, and the variable are kept to a minimum, when the simpler emotion of "true love" is involved.

A runic formula for successful love magic is made up of the staves shown in Figure 4.14. The rune count is 6 (multiple: 2 x 3). The runic total is 60 (multiple: 6 x 10). See section on numerical symbolism.

A tine should be created, perhaps using the bind rune shown in Figure 4.15. This bind rune uses the alternate form of the E-rune, ⼸.

X F Ⱶ ↑ M Þ

Figure 4.14. A runic formula for successful love magic.

Figure 4.15. Bind rune of a love-magic formula.

During the loading process each of the staves must first be carved and loaded separately, then bound together in a single field of force during the coloring phase. On the reverse side of the tine (or next to the galdrastfr, if space is a problem) the names of the persons to be brought together should be etched. This of course takes place in step three of the loading ritual. Great care should be taken to bring maximum imaginative and emotional force to bear in the identification of the *three* entities involved—the two lovers and the runic forces of attraction, binding, and love. The loaded tine could be worn by the runester to attract the lover to him/her, or it could be placed in a location near the desired one, such as under his/her bed, under or over a threshold through which the beloved one regularly passes, and so on.

An alternate form of this spell involves etching all the elements of the talismanic formula on a piece of jewelry that is then given to the future lover of the vitki. This of course may be done only in certain special circumstances. The vitki must know the desired one well enough for this to be proper and effective, and it must be known that he or she will wear or be near the object for at least some period of time. This type of rune spell also may necessitate the use of secret runic codes. The future lover might be suspicious of "mystic signs" carved on the jewel. If, for example, a medallion is the object in question, the reverse side might be encoded as shown in Figure 4.16 (See section on runic codes in Chapter 1 for further information.) The names could be inscribed using the same code in the side spaces on the rim of the form. In such cases the vitki should perform the loading ritual in the usual fashion, except that when the coded representations are etched, the rune should be strongly visualized and loaded into the numerical symbol. The imagination and talent of the runester are the only limits to the ingenuity this type of talisman may reach. But one must be strong in the basic magical skills and be very familiar with the runic system to make this type of talisman work. One of the most powerful portions of a rite of this kind is the formáli, in which a poem of true love and burning lust should be composed and loaded with passionate sexual energy.

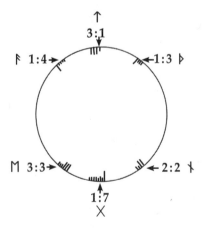

Figure 4.16. Encoded form of a love-magic formula. The markings at the top form 3:1, meaning third row first rune.

Revenge and Defense

This is called "revenge" and "defense" and not merely "curse" because it should be performed only when the vitki has been harmed in some way by the intended victim of the operation or when the victim would have harmed the vitki or his or her loved ones had the dreaded *niding* pole not been raised to crush the adversary.

The *nidhstöng* or cursing pole (literally "pole of insult or libel") is a long pole on which formulas of insult and curse are carved; then the pole is partially sunk into the ground facing toward the victim's home. The head of the pole is furnished with a horse's head or a representation of the victim in some obscene position. The sagas abound with stories about these niding poles. In order to perform a niding ritual, the vitki will need a stick or pole two feet or more in length, a sculpture of a horse's head or a carved representation of the victim. In ancient times the Ásatuár-skalds often composed niding poems and raised poles against the Christian clerics who were invading the Northland.

The pole acts as a magnet for the deadly forces of Hel which are drawn up through the pole from the subterranean streams and projected through the horse's head, or other representation, to the victim. The inscription on the pole forms the stream and gives its mission.

The actual performance of a niding-pole ritual is somewhat simpler than other talismanic operations. Find a suitable location to set up the pole (it need not be especially *near* the victim, but it is best if it is within sight of his / her / their dwelling place). Go the work-stead at midnight and perform a proper opening rite. Spend some time in meditative silence, working up your emotional power against the victim. In this state compose a prosaic or poetic runic formula of niding. An example would be:

Three thruses I threw to thee ᚦᚦᚦ
(thurisaz thurisaz thurisaz) and three
ices too ᛁᛁᛁ *(isa isa isa),* [15]
All the wild wights and all the
fierce fetches worried and warted thy
sorry soul—Hel hast thee now
(victim's name)!

Transliterate the formáli in to runes (see Appendix B) and ritually carve them into the pole. It is necessary to color only the staves : ᚦᚦᚦ :

and : ||| :. Set the figurehead on the pole and sink it into the ground repeating the niding formula. Imagine the forces of Hel—the Goddess of Death—sending forth all her might in streams of blackish (or whatever color the vitki might associate with destruction) "light" toward the doomed victim. Now the vitki should imagine the victim destroyed by the forces of Hel and returned to her dark embrace. The marked soul is smashed by the TH-runes and squashed and restricted by the I-runes. The ritual is concluded by breaking the sphere of working and projecting all residue through the figurehead to the target. Leave the pole standing until the desired result has been accomplished.

In days of yore the niding poles usually were raised against political or religious enemies rather than purely personal ones. The vitki must always ask his or her innermost self whether or not the niding pole is the right (: ℞ :) solution to the situation.

A curse also may be cast in a talismanic form that is given secretly to the victim or placed somewhere in close proximity to him/ her in much the same way the love spell works.

Draught of Wisdom

With the draught of wisdom, the vitki loads a rune tine, scrapes the runes into a drink of mead, ale, or beer, and drinks it down—rune might and all! In the sixth stanza of the "Sigrdrífumál" we read a fine example of this practice in the context of an initiatory ritual. The valkyrja Sigrdrífa, says to the hero, Sigurdhr:

> *I bring thee beer*
> *thou warrior of battle* [16]
> *blended with might*
> *and mighty renown;*
> *it is full of songs*
> *and soothing staves*
> *good magic*[17]
> *and mighty runes.*

The valkyrja then teaches the hero rune lore.

To absorb a dose of rune wisdom the vitki should duly load a rune tine according to ritual form—except do not color the runes with pigment, instead wet them with mead, ale, or beer. Also, do not carve them deeply but rather etch them lightly into the surface of the tine. After the loading is complete, take the rune knife and scrape off the runes into the cup of mead while singing a formula such as

I shave the shining runes,
and their shaping-might,
from the wood of wisdom;
into the draught they drop!

Then mix the contents well with the rune knife, while repeating a formula such as

Rune-might be mixed
with this mead of wisdom,
blended together in a bond of strength.

Now hold the cup or horn aloft with the words:

Óðhrœrir roar into the draught!

Drink the contents of the cup or horn to the dregs. During all this ritual action concentrate on the blending of forces, their vivification in the holy mead of inspiration, and your personal system and its absorption of those forces. This technique may be adopted for a variety of magical or mystical operations, and it is a potent tool in group work and initiatory rites.

Further Runic Formulas

One of the oldest and still most effective runic formulas is ALU, which appears on stones and talismans from as early as 400 CE. The word literally means "ale." *Alu* originally was a term for magical power and divine inspiration. The term was later transferred to one of the main symbols of this power and inspiration, the intoxicating brew. This power often was used to protect sacred sites from the uninitiated. The formula may be modulated in a variety of ways and may be inscribed a-1-u or u-1-a; the A-rune may fare either direction. The numerical formula also is quite potent. Figure 4.17 shows a rune count of 3 (multiple: 1 x 3 [prime]). The rune total is 27 (multiple: 3 x 9). The force of alu seems to be one of almost perpetual motions constantly turning in on itself and intensifying itself. A tine created with this formula will impart general protection, while providing wisdom, inspiration, magical power, and good health within a lawful life.

Figure 4.1 7. The ALU formula.

ᚠ ᚱ ᚢ
4. 21. 2.

The single stave that stood for the yew tree was always a powerful symbol of protection (among other things). The formula shown in figure 4.18 is a "translation" and magical adaptation of an ancient formula of yew magic. The numerical analysis reveals a rune count of 3 (multiple: 1 x 13 [prime]) and a rune total of 160 (multiple: 10 x 16). The yew force is reemphasized and brought into material manifestation.

ᚠᚷᚨᛁᚾᛋᛏᚨᛚᛖᛁᛁ:ᛋ

against al ev̂ il :ᛋ

Figure 4.18. Adaptation of an ancient formula for yew magic.

Note also the long staves on the A-runes. This distinguishes them for a particular interpretation (3 x 4 = 12), which is intended to say "the blessings of ansuz (Ódhinic force) in all three realms of being throughout the year" (:ᛟ:). If possible, this tine should be fashioned from yew wood. This formula is a good example of how much depth can be plugged into even a modern English version of a runic formula.

The following talismanic galdrastafir suggest some of the countless ways in which these bind runes may be used.

Figure 4.19. A bind rune for success. The numerical analysis is . . . ?

For general success in all the affairs of day-to-day life, the runes ᛏ ᚺ ᚦ may be combined as in Figure 4.19—a powerful formula for artists, magicians, and lovers in the realms of action, also magically powerful as an invocation of force in all Nine Worlds. Many other levels of potency also may be infused into this galdrastafr.

For obtaining justice, whether it be from a court of law or from the "court of life," use a combination of the runes ᛏ ᚱ ᛟ in the form shown in figure 4.20.

One of the more obvious cosmic and magical concerns of the runic system is that of prosperity and well-being. This is facilitated by a mighty galdrastafr made up of two F-runes, four TH-runes, and the NG- and O-runes in the symmetrical

Figure 4.20. A bind rune for justice. The numerical analysis reveals a doubling of the force of the T-rune.

configuration shown in Figure 4.21. A quick analysis by the runester reveals the many fold sources of power contained in this bind rune.

Again, it might be well to point out that in the carving and loading of such bind runes *each* intended stave must be either carved individually or reinforced within the collective configuration, and definitely they must be initially charged individually. The order of carving for the talismanic bind rune portrayed at right is shown in Figure 4.22. After the fifth stage the four TH-runes concealed in the figure should be deepened with the proper number of repetitions of the galdr.

Figure 4.21. A bind rune for prosperity and well-being.

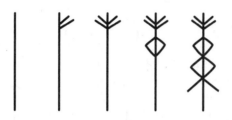

Figure 4.22. Pattern for carving a bind rune.

Death of Rune Tines

In most runic formálar not only should the definite purpose of the talismanic being be stated but also the length of time the wight is to *live*, that is, be vivified with magical force. A convenient formula for this is "until thy work is wrought." Since the wight of the tine is a living being, its death should be attended with proper ritual. This is to ensure that the magical force stored up in the form will be redirected back to its source (the vitki), or as a form of sacrifice.

There are two principal methods for effecting this important ritual act. The first emphasizes the *animate* nature of the tine wight and is modeled on funeral rites. There are two types of funeral rituals of reabsorption: cremation and burial. The former is most effective in returning the power to the personal sphere of the vitki through the heavenly streams, while the latter is a powerful way to direct the power through the chthonic streams. The second method, which emphasizes the *dynamistic* nature of the rune might, prescribes a ritual removal of the runes from the tine, using the knife. The scrapings are then burned in the brazier. (This is also a method of banishing the rune magic of another runester.) In all cases this should be done with simple dignity, attended by proper formalár of the vitki's own composition. Proper respect should be paid to the wight, the rune might, and the shaper of the tine—the vitki. This "ecology of power" is rather like the ancient Norse lore of rebirth, which postulates that the innate might of the ancestors is continually reformed in the descendants.

Stadhagaldr

This discipline is heavily indebted to the work of twentieth-century runic magicians of Germany who developed a system they call *Runenyoga*. In the writings of Siegfried Adolf Kummer, Friedrich Bernhard Marby, and Karl Spiesberger there is much concerning *Runen-Asana, Runen-mudra*, and so on. Indeed, they seem a bit too dependent on the kindred Indian discipline. Nevertheless, their practical experiments, invaluable clues, and ritual formulas are the basis for the following work.

Theory and Use

In comparison to what yoga became in later centuries, stadhagaldr is an active system of magic that consists of the assumption of runic postures or gestures for magical effect, both within the vitki and in his or her environment. Both systems are most probably derived from the same common Indo-European root tradition of magical and symbolic gestures.

Gestures and postures form some part of almost every metaphysical or magical school. They can be seen from the simple folding of hands in prayer to the extremely complex system of *asanas* in the Indian *hatha yoga* school. Stadhagaldr is balanced in this respect. The number and intricacy of the postures are varied enough to be expressive of the wide variety of forces present, but none require extensive training or straining of the body. The great advantage of stadhagaldr in the runic system is that it allows the actual shape of the stave to be embodied in the physical apparatus of the vitki. This can result in the embodiment of the entire runic mystery in the flesh of the vitki, thereby turning the body into an awesome magical tool! The overall aims of stadhagaldr are:

1. Control of the body through posture (stadha)

2. Control of thought through song (galdr)

3. Control of breath

4. Control of emotion

5. Becoming aware of the rune realms of the self and of the world(s)

6. Control and direction of the will

Each of these aims should be striven for in turn, until all six have been mastered.

It must be stressed vigorously that the body should not be viewed as something evil or as an enemy to be defeated or whipped into submission but rather as a source for great and holy energy, obtainable through no other medium, if only directed in harmony with the hugr. The body is the vitki's personal portion of Midhgardhr, the balanced center of the multiverse containing the potential of all the worlds.

Stadhagaldr is used as a mode of psychological integration and personal transmutation, and it is also employed in *all* other types of magical operations. The vitki may, for example, literally build a numinous, living runic talisman within the body through stadhagaldr, so that he or she *becomes a walking rune* line. The principles of runic combination and blending work with stadhagaldr in exactly the same way they function with the tine or sign magic. The stödhur are just an alternate mode of expression for the rune might.

Intake of World and Earth Streams

The practice of this magical form is closely connected to the mysteries of the rune streams. The runic postures act as antennas of force by which the vitki may attract, modulate, and re-project rune might for magical purposes.

As the vitki knows, there are three types of rune streams: the heavenly, the terrestrial, and the subterranean or chthonic. The heavenly *and* chthonic streams are world or cosmic streams and are not peculiar to this planet, as are the terrestrial streams that flow just under and above the surface of the earth. The individual self contains counterparts to each of these streams, which act as a matrix through which the rune streams act upon and affect us. These streams are perceived in many different ways: some are vibrations; others are waves, flows, rays, and even contractions. The induction of these forces is the mainstay of stadhagaldr.

Power is actually drawn in through the hands and/or feet and head, directly to the central axis of the vitki. There it is absorbed and modulated, then reemitted for specific purposes or assimilated to alter the self of the vitki. Each runic posture receives and transmits force in a particular pattern, and from various realms, according to its shape. This power is directly connected to the physical world through the medium of the hu man nervous system. When performing the various rune stodhur, the vitki should visualize and *feel* the flows of force being gathered or projected in a particular pat tern through the body, which is in the form of the stave. This will feel as if electric current is passing through your body and will appear as rays of light coursing in angular patterns. Each individual vitki should let personal experience take precedence over anything read in this or any other book. Personal feelings and reactions, rather than "logical" thought processes, are more effective guidelines in the realm of practical magic. This is especially true in stadhagaldr.

Table 4.4 shows four examples of rune shapes, their patterns of power, and the realms of being they engage, and may give some practical hints for more fruitful development. The arrows indicate the directions in which the force streams. These are based on personal practice and observation and should in no way be taken as dogma. Notice that the diagonals sometimes feel as if they were terrestrial links and sometimes as if they were links to the heavenly or subterranean realms. This is true even with the same rune on different occasions, for the rune world is hardly a static one. A good rune vitki will attempt to experience all of these forces empirically, and with increased skill he or she will then begin to divide and classify the raw forces into their finer runic characteristics. With proper and persistent practice empirical results will arise.

Table 4.4. Some Patterns of Force Streams

	Subterranean streams are lifted into the vitki and circulate back to their source.
	Heavenly and subterranean forces flow into vitki. There they are synthesized and sent out into the terrestrial realm as manifest action.
	A crosscurrent of directed terrestrial force flows through the vertical axis of world streams, resulting in a concentrated intensification of power at the point of confluence.
	Heavenly and subterranean streams are received and assimilated, and all are redirected toward the heavenly realm.

The ancient vitkar knew well the power of the earth streams, for they formed one of their mightiest mysteries. The best work-stead for stadhagaldr is a known "power point" where the earth and world streams (the horizontal and vertical) flow together. These are known by all cultures all over the world. The vitki should seek these out for important rites of stadhagaldr.

The human being is constantly being bombarded by power flowing from above, below, and from all corners of the earth; the task is to control this influx and direct it. We receive the power of brightness from the wide expanse of space, and we induct the constricting force of darkness churning in the center of the earth. It is most important that we realize *both* extremes and consciously seek them out, develop them to their limits, and center them in our consciousness.

Before attempting any practical magical work in this system, the stödhur of all the runes to be used in the operation should be mastered through an intense program of meditational exercise with the runic postures in question.

Opening Formula in *Stadhagaldr*

A work of stadhagaldr may begin with the general opening rite given in the section on talismanic magic, or the vitki may use a special *stadhasetning* (posture rite) for engaging the runic forces. This is a powerful rite with which to practice stadhagaldr, and therefore these three stödhur should perhaps be mastered first. Here, as in the following rites, a stave presented beside a galdr formáli indicates that the vitki should assume the stadha of the rune and sing its formulaic galdr and/or the formáli that loads the ritual actions with more refined intentions (see Table 4.5).

Table 4.5. Stödhur for Engaging Runic Forces

I	*Self-knowing, I am a staff* *for beams and waves of rune might.*
ᚾ	*Self-knowing, I shape the might* *from the deepest depths* *out of the realms of the earth* *out of the womb of Hel (or the earth mother).*
ᛉ	*Self-knowing, I shape the might* *from the highest heights* *out of the wide world* *out of Heimdallr's realm.*

Simple Rites

The performance of any single rune stadha may of course be considered a rite. This is especially true if the vitki composes a formáli to be recited after the galdr is sung. This formáli will give specific shape and purpose to the runic force engendered by the operation. The possibilities for potent works of simple beauty are almost limitless. The following rites of combined runic forces are essentially made up of several of these simpler rites blended together to form a more complex magical effect. They describe flows or processes of power aimed toward a specific goal, such as Increase in Magical Power (Table 4.6), Success and Victory (Table 4.7), Increase in Creative Force (Table 4.8). Table 4 .9 is a Rite of Need. The advantage of stadha-ritual work is that it provides keys to various realms of consciousness, and it inspires the vitki to the greatest power, if properly performed on all levels of being.

Our aim in the rites of stadhagaldr is the blending of several runic forces into one single concentrated and directed stream of power with a definite goal or aim. This is to be achieved by combining the forms and sounds of various runes together into a single force field of action. The symbol of the operation may be a series of runes or a bind rune drawn on the floor or ground or on a board lying on the altar or hung at eye level on the wall in front of the vitki This form should be the focal point of concentration throughout the entire ritual.

These ritual formulas also may be adapted as talismanic or sign-magical rites.

Table 4.6. Increase in Magical Power

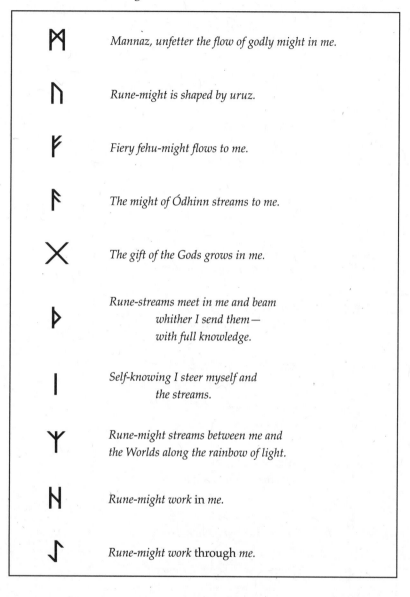

ᛗ	*Mannaz, unfetter the flow of godly might in me.*
ᚢ	*Rune-might is shaped by uruz.*
ᚠ	*Fiery fehu-might flows to me.*
ᚨ	*The might of Ódhinn streams to me.*
ᚷ	*The gift of the Gods grows in me.*
ᚦ	*Rune-streams meet in me and beam whither I send them — with full knowledge.*
ᛁ	*Self-knowing I steer myself and the streams.*
ᛉ	*Rune-might streams between me and the Worlds along the rainbow of light.*
ᚺ	*Rune-might work in me.*
ᛋ	*Rune-might work through me.*

Table 4.7. Success and Victory

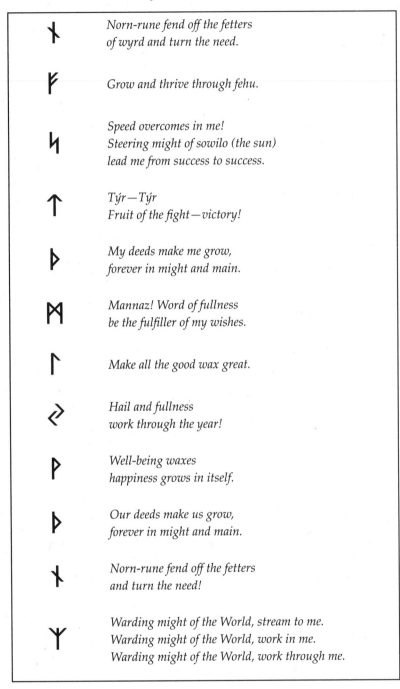

ᛉ   *Norn-rune fend off the fetters*
        of wyrd and turn the need.

ᚠ   *Grow and thrive through fehu.*

ᛋ   *Speed overcomes in me!*
        Steering might of sowilo (the sun)
        lead me from success to success.

ᛏ   *Týr—Týr*
        Fruit of the fight—victory!

ᚦ   *My deeds make me grow,*
        forever in might and main.

ᛗ   *Mannaz! Word of fullness*
        be the fulfiller of my wishes.

ᛚ   *Make all the good wax great.*

ᛃ   *Hail and fullness*
        work through the year!

ᚹ   *Well-being waxes*
        happiness grows in itself.

ᚦ   *Our deeds make us grow,*
        forever in might and main.

ᛉ   *Norn-rune fend off the fetters*
        and turn the need!

ᛦ   *Warding might of the World, stream to me.*
        Warding might of the World, work in me.
        Warding might of the World, work through me.

Table 4.8. Increase in Creative Force

Rune	Text
ᚠ	*Fiery fehu-might flows to me.*
ᚢ	*Uruz shapes the rune-might.*
ᚦ	*Rune-streams meet in me and beam whither I send them.*
ᚨ	*The might of my word waxes.*
ᚱ	*On the right road I wander.*
ᚲ	*Skill comes to me through the might of kenaz knowledge and World-wisdom wax in me through kenaz.*
ᛋ	*The speed of sowilo (the sun) steers me.*
ᛏ	*Týr—Týr Will of speedy shaping successfully stream through me.*
ᛃ	*Hail and fullness— gifts of the good year!*

Table 4.9. Rite of Need

Norn-rune fend off the fetters of
    wyrd, turn the need.
    Thou art my need—
    through thee I overcome need.

Wight of the World—wood
    give good speed and help!
    I take up the runes,
    I take up my need!

Need-fire flame in me!

Mannaz! Word of fullness
    be the fulfiller of my needs
    and unfetter the flow of rune-might.

Rune-might streams between me
    and the worlds
    along the rainbow of light.

Need-fire flame in me!

Steering might of the sun
    lead me forward.

Need-fire flame in me! (Repeat this until the fire is
enkindled in your breast.)

The Ritual Talisman

Whether or not the vitki is performing a talismanic loading ritual, a symbol describing the particular runic operation may be formed to serve as a lasting outward symbol of the holy inner process that takes place in the rite. This is usually a bind rune or rune row, which is incised into or painted on a board or paper. This should be displayed in some place where the vitki will see it regularly and thus constantly reaffirm his or her link to the magical force. It also may be portrayed on a small object the vitki carries.

This technique should be used only in cases where the vitki desires to effect an internal change in his or her own consciousness. For operations that intend to affect the outside environment the vitki should expend all possible energy during the ritual, then make a complete break with the force, thus releasing it to do its work. In the latter case a constant reminder would only hinder the successful fulfillment of the vitki's will.

Sign Magic

The practice of sign magic involves the blending of the techniques of signing and sending with those of galdr (incantation). This form of magic is the most difficult because it requires the greatest amount of concentration and visualization to be maximally effective. Once the techniques have been mastered, however, it promises to be the most direct and effective form of galdr available to the vitki. The techniques of signing and sending already have been mastered, and the vitki is by now quite familiar with several aspects of incantation. Here we will deepen this knowledge and direct it in more specific technical channels toward formulating the basis of *signingagaldr* (the magic of signs). The main difference between the signing found in this section and that used in the loading of tines is that here the signs are directed toward and melded with already living systems, be they wights or dynamistic fields of runic force.

The idea behind sign magic is that the vitki actually may cut runes into the living fabric of the multiverse, melding that rune might with a symbolic "target" that has been formulated by the hugr of the vitki through concentrated visualization, thus bringing about a change in that target. This is only one of many ways to use the techniques of sign magic. This process may be carried out in the hugauga (totally by meditative visualization) or by external ritual work. In both cases the techniques are the same; however, the vitki may wish to begin with the visualization method and work into more difficult ceremonial performance.

The three steps necessary to signingagaldr are (1) the formulation of and/or concentration on a target, (2) the formulation and projection of the willed rune might, and (3) the melding of the previous two into a single field of force such that the second influences the first in the desired way.

To formulate a target for the projected magical force, the vitki will need to set off a "target area." This is a framework within which the visualized target is held, so that the rune might may be directed into it. This may be either rectangular or triangular in shape. If a triangle is used, the form ▷ is preferred. In full ritual work a frame may be constructed from wood and suitably painted or otherwise decorated. The frame may contain a symbol form of the target (a picture, for example), but most often the vitki will magically build the form of the target image within the framework using his or her powers of concentration and visualization.

Once the target is firmly established and bound within the frame, the vitki begins to formulate the willed rune might in the center of his or her body. This power is then projected into the target area and signed in the manner described in the section on sending and signing. The galdr and/or formáli that is sung or spoken should give intention and refined form to the runic power. As the runester signs the rune, it should be as if the force of the sign was actually being infused into the living fabric of the target. The vitki will immediately *see* the change in the target once the melding of forces is complete.

Although the practice of sending and signing is fairly well known by now, the use of galdr perhaps needs more development in the context of sign magic. Throughout this book *we* have seen both the sound-for-mulaic and poetic forms of galdrar. In sign magic both forms may be used, but the vitki should always aim for the more complex poetic form because of the degree of flexibility and exactness that it affords. These "magic songs" are found throughout old Germanic literatures, and indeed for the ancient Teutons (as well as all other Indo-European peoples) the art of poetry grew out of the power of magic.

The galdr serves to aid in the invocation/evocation of the rune might and in its formation within the vitki. But it also aids in projection and linkage of that force to the target through its principal quality—vibration.

The following techniques should be followed throughout the practice of sending and signing, for all the elements mentioned in this section must be understood as the multifold expression of a single force—the will of the runester. The breath should be the focal point of concentration throughout the galdr. During inhalations the vitki concentrates on the flow of rune might into the personal center. There it is momentarily held for exact formulation, and then, on exhalation, the portion of the galdr that is to be projected is intensely concentrated on. Most galdrar of all types require several breaths to perform completely. One line of the incantation may be performed with each breath. In the case of poetic galdrar the vitki should "runically" concentrate on each letter-sound of every word in the incantation-feeling their force. Do not necessarily *think* about their meaning; if it is well composed, the galdr will seem to do its own work. What is important here is the flow of force, its formulation, and its projection in a smooth concentrated pattern that becomes almost unconscious to the accomplished vitki. A unity is built between the rune might, the vitki, and the target in such a way that the special nature of this magical form soon becomes apparent.

The main magical unity on which the runester must consciously concentrate is that of the *sound* (of the incantation) and the *form* (of the stave and the beam of light through which it is projected), all within the common "runic vibration." Meditational exercises will greatly aid in this process. Incantations may be sung either out loud or within the hugr. Also, when they are spoken out loud, the galdrar may be sonorously and boomingly sung or softly whispered. The former seems more effective when the vitki is performing a rite in solitude or in the company of fellow vitkar, while the latter is often more powerful when non-vitkar are present.

Because this form of galdr comes so close to an unconscious, meditational approach, it is most necessary to *memorize* all aspects of the rite before it is performed. This is generally a good suggestion for all rites, but it is especially necessary here. A successful try at signingagaldr is dependent on a curious and magnificent blend of all segments of the runester's psychosomatic complex. The unexpected mystical "fringe benefits" of these operations are often astounding.

Perhaps a further note should be added concerning poetic galdrar. These certainly may be composed in English. (See Appendix D for technical suggestions in this matter.) Much thought should go into their composition as to both form and content. The dedicated vitki will undertake the study of Old Norse and/or other old Germanic dialects (e.g., Old English, Gothic, and Old High German), for these languages vibrate with magico-mythic qualities that are hard to conjure up in Modern English. But what is most important is that the vitki find a magically potent language and poetic form that speaks with the voice of his or her unconscious realms.

Other Forms of Magic

The runic system encompasses several areas that because of the scope of this book have been impractical to address fully. However, their existence and some of their characteristics should be pointed out so that anyone entering the rune world will know some of the vastness of the system, and it is hoped this will lead to further investigations by talented vitkar throughout the world.

Divination is a well-attested use of rune lore in ancient times, and it is an art widely practiced by modern vitkar. The knowledgeable vitkar may make a beginning in this area by learning the "language of the runes" first, then applying this knowledge in a very simple technique outlined by Tacitus in the *Germania*. This method may be utilized in the following manner by the modern rune vitki. First, ritually construct twenty-four rune lots (hlutar) from oak or beech wood, each loaded with a different rune of the Elder Futhark. These lots are most convenient when made of flat thin strips of wood, such as a veneer, about one inch by two inches. Also, procure a white linen cloth, about three feet by three feet. At an auspicious time, and preferably outside, spread the cloth on the ground with its flat edges directed to the four quarters. Stand near its southern edge, facing north, and shuffle the lots while concentrating on the subject of the divination. With the lots held in your hands, stand in the Y stadha and concentrate on the question or problem. Once a firm link has been established, sing the galdr:

Rúnar rádha rétt rádh![18]
(Runes rown right rede!)

Then throw the lots onto the cloth, repeating the Nornic names:

Urdhr — Verdhandi — Skuld!

before the lots hit the cloth. Close your eyes and walk up to the cloth. Randomly pick up three lots. The first indicates the past or root of the matter, the second illuminates the present condition, and the third reveals what *should* come about, given the other two factors. (See the P-rune.)

Other forms of galdr also are contained in the runic system. Much of this is bound up with the liturgical forms of Ásatrú. Oath magic, involves swearing oaths on sacred objects such as the altar ring or a sacrificial animal, is one of these forms. God, goddesses, other wights, and aspects of the personal soul may also be invoked/evoked to communicate with the hugr of the vitki; however, these forms belong more properly to the function of the *erilaz*. There also are several types of initiation that are proper to the life of the vitki and/or erilaz.

Seidhr is a magical form independent of runic symbolism, but it can be made an integral part of the rune world. The Ynglinga Saga reports how Ódhinn was taught the art of seidhr by its mistress, Freyja. Seidhr includes the techniques of shape shifting, "soul" projection, traveling through the worlds, sex magic, and other procedures that have a what some people consider a shamanistic character. Reading through the Eddas and sagas, the vitki will find many inspirational examples of these, and many other fascinating forms of magic.

• • •

In the original edition of this book, the manuscript for which I finished in 1979, I included, without further commentary, the following original poem— really a rune-spell cast out upon the world at that time. I think it is a good example of how to work the magic of the runes. *Reyn til Rúna!*

Wide stands the door
to the rune-worlds' winds
loud ring their songs'
sounds through the northern night:
the wise wend their way toward might and main,
again to learn that holy lore.

The sun-born sisters
and brothers bright
call in their night of need:
staves strong and holy
in rune-might standing
enkindle the craft
and cunning ways
to win weal and wisdom.

On a shining plain
runesters ply their skill
in a Gard of the Gods
in the northern light—
the runes bloom forth,
roaring their songs,
through a house all whole,
again as aye anon.

APPENDIX A

Pronunciations of Old Norse

The phonetic values provided below also serve as a convenient guide to
the phonetics of the galdrar.
The consonants *b, d, f, k, l, m, n, t,* and *v* are just as in Modern English.

a	as in "artistic"	ey	pronounced same as *ei*
á	as in "father"	g	always hard as in "go"
e	as in "men"	ng	as in "long"
é	as u in German *"See"*	h	same as English except
	(as *ay* in "bay")		before consonants, then as
i	as in "it"		*wh* in "where"
í	as *ee* in "feet"	j	always as *y* in "year"
o	as in "omit"	p	as in English, except before
ó	as in "ore"		*i* then this pt cluster is
ö	(also written *o*) as *o* in "not"		pronounced *ft*
ϕ	pronounced same as ö	r	trilled *r*
u	as in "put"	s	always voiceless as in "sing"
ú	as in "rule"	th	in initial position voiceless
æ	as *ai* in "hair"		*th* as in "thin"
œ	as *u* in "slur"	dh	medially and in final
y	as *u* in German *"Hütte"* (*i*		position voiced *th* as in
	with rounded lips) "		"the"
ý	as *u* in German *"Tur"* (*ee*	rl	pronounced *dl*
	with rounded lips)	rn	pronounced *dn*
au	as *ou* in "house"	nn	pronounced *dn* after long
ei	as *ay* in "May, or *i* in "mine"		vowels and diphthongs

APPENDIX B

On the Transliteration of Modern English into Runes

This topic poses some problems, especially when it comes to putting proper names into runic form. The correspondences reviewed below will provide ample guidelines, but the vitki should let intuition and magical criteria be the final arbiter. In some cases, it may be found best to go with the actual English *sound* rather than the literal correspondences.

In writing poetry of your own composition in runes it will be found most convenient if you stick to Anglo-Saxon roots (see Appendix C). Questions of "correctness" in transliteration are fewer when Germanic words are used.

This chart shows the best way to use the Elder Futhark to write in runes. One might also consider using the Ango-Saxon Futhorc for this, as it is a system created for English, after all, albeit *Old* English. For more details on the topic of writing in runes, see my little book *Rune-Writing: Our Original Way of Writing and the Key to Learning to Write Modern English in Anglo-Saxon Runes* (Runestar, 2020).

A	ᚠ	K	ᚲ	T	ᛏ
B	ᛒ	L	ᛚ	U	ᚢ
C	ᚲ	M	ᛗ	V	ᚢ or ᚠ
D	ᛞ	N	ᚾ	W	ᚹ
E	ᛖ	O	ᛟ	X	ᚲᚺ (k + s)
F	ᚠ	P	ᛈ	Y	ᛇ
G	ᚷ	Q	ᚲ	Z	ᛋ or ᛉ
H	ᚺ	R	ᚱ (ᛉ in final	TH	ᚦ / ᛞ (voiceless/
I	ᛁ or ᛁ		position)		voiced)
J	ᛁ or ᛇ	S	ᛋ	NG	◇

APPENDIX C

On Poetics

Poetry is a potent tool of magical technique that should never be ignored by any vitki. To the ancient Germanic peoples the poet was a magical figure, and *skáldakraft* (the power of poetry) was a magical force. Poetry *shapes* magical forces contained in the world according to the will of its "creator." Remember, Ódhinn is the god of the runes, magic, and poetry (among other things).

Each vitki should choose a poetic form with which he or she feels most comfortable and effective. This may be executed in English or some other "ritual language." Old English, with Old Norse, gives us the most elegant examples of old Germanic verse forms, but this great and native power has been suppressed by non-English forms from French and Latin. Here I would like to point out some of the possibilities for composing Germanic-style poetry in Modern English.

The most important element of composing Germanic style verse is vocabulary choice. Through the centuries English has become more and more infused with Latin and Greek derivatives that speak clearly to the intellect but are dumbfounded before the soul. Therefore, it is most effective to try to choose Modern English words with Anglo-Saxon or Norse (there are *many)* roots. Any dictionary with etymologies will be helpful in this regard.

This type of poetry *may* rhyme but not necessarily. The oldest form of Germanic verse used stave rhyme (alliteration) only. The verse form is based on the unit of the half line. Examples of original magical verse found throughout this book will be of some help. The most inspirational aid in this study is Professor Lee M. Hollander's translation of the *Poetic Edda* (also the introduction to that work).

APPENDIX D

Tables of Runic Correspondences

The following tables are intended to serve as guides to further rune understanding as well as stimulation toward further runic investigation by all vitkar. These correspondences are not absolute or dogmatic—as always the intuition of the vitki is the most reliable guide. Many of the correspondences will be helpful in the construction of rituals, talismans, and so on. Table A on pp. 150–151 concerns runes 1 through 24 of the Elder Futhark, with the corresponding runes of the Younger Futhark and the Armanen Futhork. This table provides a full range of correspondences, which are partially traditional and partially based upon previous twentieth century research. These columns will be found to contain many valuable theses for thought stimulus. It should be noted that all correspondences are based on the order and number of the Elder Futhark and that in the case of the younger rows the numbers in parentheses indicate positions with respect to the elder row. Table B on p. 152 provides a partial list of basic correspondences for the Anglo-Saxon runes 25 through 33.

Table A. Table of Runic Correspondences

I	II	III	IV	V	VI	VII	VIII	IX
No.	Elder Form	Elder Name	A-S Form	A-S Name	Younger Form	Younger Name	Armanen Form	Armanen Name
1	ᚠ	fehu	ᚠ	feoh	ᚠ	fé	ᚠ	fa
2	ᚢ	uruz	ᚢ	úr	ᚢ	úr	ᚢ	ur
3	ᚦ	thurisaz	ᚦ	thorn	ᚦ	thurs	ᚦ	thorn
4	ᚨ	ansuz	ᚩ	ós	ᚫ	áss	ᚩ	os
s	ᚱ	raidho	ᚱ	rád	ᚱ	reidh	ᚱ	rit
6	ᚲ	kenaz	ᚻ	cén	ᚴ	kaun	ᚴ	ka
7	ᚷ	gebo	ᚷ	gyfu	ᚼ (9)	hagall	ᚼ (9)	hagal
8	ᚹ	wunjo	ᚹ	wynn	ᚾ (10)	naudhr	ᚾ (10)	not
9	ᚺ	hagalaz	ᚾ	hægl	ᛁ (11)	íss	ᛁ (11)	is
10	ᚾ	naudhiz	ᚾ	nýd	ᚼ (12)	ár	ᛀ (12)	ar
11	ᛁ	isa	ᛁ	ís	ᛋ (16)	sól	ᛋ (16)	sig
12	ᛃ	jera	ᛄ	gér	ᛏ (17)	Týr	ᛏ (17)	tyr
13	ᛇ	eihwaz	ᛇ	éoh	ᛒ (18)	bjarkan	ᛒ (18)	bar
14	ᛈ	perdhro	ᛈ	peordh	ᛉ (20)	madhr	ᛚ (21)	laf
15	ᛉ	elhaz	ᛉ	eolh	ᛚ (21)	lögr	ᛉ (20)	man
16	ᛋ	sowilo	ᛋ	sigil	ᛦ (13)	yr	ᛦ (13)	yr
17	ᛏ	tiwaz	ᛏ	ír			ᛖ (19)	eh
18	ᛒ	berkano	ᛒ	beorc			(7)	gibor
19	ᛗ	ehwaz ehwo	ᛗ	eh				
20	ᛗ	mannaz	ᛗ	mann				
21	ᛚ	laguz laukaz	ᛚ	lagu				
22	◊	ingwaz	ᛝ	Ing				
23	ᛞ	dagaz	ᛞ	dæg				
24	ᛟ	othala	ᛟ	éthel				

Table A. Table of Runic Correspondences (Cont.)

X Tree	XI Herb	XII God/Goddess/ Wight(s)	XIII Color	XIV Astrology	XV Tarot
elder	nettle	Æsir	light red	♈	The Tower
birch	sphagnum moss	Vanir	dark green	♉	High Priestess
oak	houseleek	Thórr	bright red	♂	The Emperor
ash	fly agric	Ódhinn	dark blue	☿	Death
oak	mugwort	Forseti, Freyja	bright red	♐	The Hierophant
pine	cowslip	dwarves	light red	♀	The Chariot
ash & elm	heartsease	Ódhinn/ Freyja	deep blue	♓	The Lovers
ash	flax	Freyr, elves	yellow	♌	Strength
yew or ash	lily of the valley	Ymir	light blue	≈	The World
beech	bistort	Nornir, etins	black	♑	The Devil
alder	henbane	rime-thurses	black	☽	The Hermit
oak	rosemary	Freyr	light blue	✳	The Fool
yew	mandrake	Ódhinn/Ullr	dark blue	♏	The Hanged Man
beech	aconite	Nornir	black	♄	Wheel of Fortune
yew	angelica	valkyrjur	gold	♋	The Moon
juniper	mistletoe	Sól	white/silver	☉	The Sun
oak	sage	Týr, Mani	bright red	♎	Justice
birch	lady's mantle	Frigg; Nethus; Hel	dark green	♍	The Empress
oak, ash	ragwort	Freyja/Freyr; Alcis	white	♊	The Lovers
holly	madder	Heimdallr/ Ódhinn	deep red	♃	The Magician
willow	leek	Njördhr, Baldr	deep green	☽	The Star
apple	self-heal	Ing, Freyr	yellow	●	Judgment
spruce	clary	Ódhinn/Ostara	light blue	◐◑	Temperance
hawthorn	gold-thread	Ódhinn/Thórr	deep yellow	○	The Moon

Table B. Extended Anglo-Saxon Runic Correspondences

1 Number	II A-S Name	III A-S Form	IV Phonetic Value	V Translation	VI Esoteric
25	ác	ᚪ	a	oak tree	sacred oak
26	æsc	ᚫ	a in "at"	ash tree	primal human material
27	ýr	ᛡ	u	gold decoration	primal being
28	ior	ᛇ	io	serpent	Midhgardh- serpent
29	éar	ᛠ	ao or ea	earth-grave	ritual interment
30	cweorth	ᛣ	qu	fire-twirl	ritual fire
31	calc	ᛤ	k	chalk or cup	ritual container
32	stán	ᛥ	st	stone	altar stone
33	gár	ᚸ	g	spear	Ódhinn's spear

Glossary

Æsir: sg. Áss, genitive pl. Ása (used as a prefix to denote that the god or goddess is "of the Æsir"). ON. Race of gods corresponding to the functions of magic, law, and war.

ætt: pl. *ættrir* ON. Family or genus, used both as a name for the threefold divisions of the futhark, and the eight divisions of the heavens. Also means a group or division of *eight*.

aettir: sg. *átt.* ON. The divisions of the futhark into three "families" or "eights."

Armanen: pl. Name of the group built around the ideology of the German mystic Guido von List (1848–1919).

Ásatrú: ON. Religion *(trú)* of the Æsir. Now a name used by Norse oriented Neo-Germanic religious groups.

bind rune: Two or more runes superimposed over one another, sometimes used to form *galdraslafir.*

Edda: ON. Word of uncertain origin, used as the title of ancient manuscripts dealing with "mythology." The *Elder* or *Poetic Edda* is a collection of poems composed between 800 and 1270 CE, while the *Younger* or *Prose Edda* was written by Snorri Sturluson in 1222 as a codification of the mythology of Ásatrú for skalds.

ek vitki: ON. Statement of identity by the rune magician meaning "I (am) a person of knowledge."

erilaz: pl. *eriloz* . GMC. A vitki and runemaster who is also a priest *(godhi).*

etin: Developed from ON *jötunn.* A type of giant renowned for strength. Also, a generic giant name (in ON Jötunheimr, etc.)

fate: See *ørlög.*

formáli: pl. *formálar.* ON. Formulaic speech used to load action with magical intent.

fylfot: An archaic English designation for the swastika or solar wheel.

fylgja: pl. *fylgjur.* ON. The "fetch," a numinous being attached to every individual, which is the repository of all past action and which accordingly affects the person's life. Visualized as either a feminine form, an animal, or an abstract shape.

galdr: pl. *galdrar* ON. Originally "incantation" (the verb *gala* is also used for "to crow"); later meant magic in general.

galdrastafr: pl. *galdrastafir.* ON. Literally, "stave of incantations." A magic sign of various types, made up of bind runes, pictographs and / or ideographs.

gandr: ON. Projected magical power and the wand, staff, or stave which contains or expresses it.

Germanic: (1) The proto-language spoken by the Germanic peoples before the various dialects (e.g., English, German, Gothic, Scandi navian) developed; also, a collective term for the languages belonging to this group. (2) A collective term for all peoples descended from the Germanic-speaking group (e.g., the English, the Germans, the Scandinavians). Norse or Nordic is a subset of Germanic and refers only to the Scandinavian branch of the Germanic heritage.

glódhker: ON. Fire-pot or brazier used in magical rites. glyph runes: See *galdraslafr.*

Gothic: Designation of a now extinct East Germanic language and the people who spoke it. Last speakers known in the Crimean in the eighteenth century.

hamingja: pl. *hamingjur.* ON. Mobile magical force rather like the *maria* and *manilu* of other traditions. Often defined as "luck," "shape-shifting force," and "guardian spirit."

hamr: ON. The plastic image-forming substance that surrounds each individual, making up the physical form. It may be collected and reformed by magical power *(hamingja)* according to the will *(hugr).*

"Hávamál": ON. "Sayings of the High One." The second poem of the *Elder Edda;* it contains words of wisdom, initiatory myths, and magical songs.

Hel: ON. (1) The abode of the dead at the root of the world-tree. (2) The goddess of the dead and death.

holy sign: See *galdrastafr.*

hlutr: ON. "Lot." A piece of wood with a rune carved on it for use in religious or divinatory workings.

hugr: ON. A portion of the psychosomatic complex corresponding to the conscious mind, intellect, will.

hugauga: ON. The "mind's eye" a spiritual *hvel* in the forehead.

hvel: pl. *hvel.* ON. Literally, this means "wheel" (analogous to the Sanskrit *ćakra)*, a spiritual center in the human body where magical forces are collected, transformed, and either assimilated or projected.

madhr: pl. *menn.* ON. "Man."

multiverse: A term descriptive of the *many* states of being (worlds) that constitute the universe. The word is a play on universe (onebeing). *Multiverse* is used when emphasis is placed upon the multiplicity of being, while *universe* is used for a unitary emphasis.

niding: Developed from the ON words *nídh* (insult) and *nídhingr* (a vile wretch). Used in the context of cursing by the use of satirical or insulting poetry.

Norn: pl. Nornir. ON. One of the three complex cosmic beings in female form that embody the processes of cause and effect and evolutionary force.

numen: adj. numinous. Living, nonphysical, or magical aspects within the cosmic order, not necessarily meant in the animistic sense; that which partakes of this spiritual power.

ódhrœrir: ON. Exciter or stirrer of inspiration. This is both a name of the magico-poetic mead and its container.

Old English: The language spoken by the Anglo-Saxon tribes in southern Britain from about 450–1100 CE. Also known as Anglo-Saxon.

Old Norse: The language spoken by West Scandinavians (in Norway, Iceland, and Britain) in the Viking Age (c. 800–1100 CE). Also, the language of the Eddas and of skaldic poetry.

önd: ON. Vital breath.

ørlög: ON. Literally analyzed, this means "primal layers" (primal laws) i.e., the past action (of an individual or the cosmos) that shapes the present and future conditions. Roughly translated as "fate." Root concept of the English "weird" *(wyrd).*

ristir: ON. Tool used for carving runes.

runagaldrar: ON. "Rune-magic."

runester: Term based on the ON term *rýnstr,* "one most skilled in runes," but used as a general term for one who knows or deals with runes. Also called "runer."

seidhr: ON. A form of Norse magic often contrasted with galdr. Seidhr involves attaining trance states.

sign: See *signing.*

signing: pl. *signingar.* ON. Magical signs or gestures made with motions of the hands to trace various magical symbols in the air around an object or person to be affected by their power.

"Sigrdrifumál": A poem of the *Elder Edda* in which the hero, Sigurdhr (Siegfried), is initia ted into rune wisdom by the valkyrja, Sigrdrífa. The title means "The Sayings of Sigrdrífa."

skald: ON term for a poet who composes highly formal, originally magical verse.

stadha: pl. *stödhur.* ON. A position or posture of the body, etc.

stadhagaldr: ON. "Posture magic": the magical technique of assuming runic postures coupled with incantational formulas.

stave: (1) A stick or wand of wood upon which runes are carved. (2) A general alternative term to "rune" itself.

taufr: ON. Talismanic magic, a talisman.

thurs: From the ON *thurs*, pl. *thursar.* Giants renowned for their witlessness and strength.

tine: Developed from the ON word *teinn* (talisman).

valkyrja: pl. *valkyrjur.* ON. "Chooser of the fallen" (i.e., the slain). Protective *fylgja*-like numinous qualities that become attached to certain persons who attract them; a linking force between men and gods (especially Ódhinn).

Vanir: sg. Van. ON. The race of gods corresponding to the fertility function. The principal deities of this group are Freyja, Freyr, and Njördhr. After a long war with the Æsir, they all exchanged hostages and lived in peace. The Vanir who came to the Æsir camp became assimilated into the Æsir, while retaining their special characteristics.

vé: ON. "Sacred enclosure": the place of working magic. The name of Ódhinn's "brother."

vitki: pl. vitkar. ON. (Used throughout this book as if English.) "Magician, wise one": a magician and one versed in rune lore, who is not necessarily a *godhi* (priest) within the Faith of the Æsir but who remains within the natural laws of that Faith.

"Völuspá": ON. "Prophecy of the Seeress." The first song in the *Elder Edda,* it deals with cosmogony, anthropogony, and eschatology.

wight: Archaic English for a living being of any kind. (OE. with)

World: (1) The entire cosmos or universe. (2) One of the nine levels of being or planes of existence that make up the ordered cosmos.

World-Tree: See Yggdrasill.

Yggdrasil: ON. The cosmic tree of nine worlds or planes of the multiverse.

Notes

1. The use of the term *holistic* deserves some comment here. It is interesting to note that the Germanic idea of "holy" is identical to that embodied in *holistic*; i.e., the wholeness, completeness, and unity of all realms, leading to well-being. The English words *holy*, *hale*, and *whole* all derive from the same root: **kailo-* (whole, uninjured, of good omen).

2. In the old Germanic languages, before they were touched by Christian influence, the word *god* (ON *godh*) was neuter. After male-dominated Christian dogma was infused into the language, the gender of the word was changed to masculine.

3. A literal translation of this phrase would be "Hammer in the North hallow this sacred enclosure and keep watch (over it)!"

4. This version is poetically more effective and therefore better for those wishing to use English in their rites.

5. "The Awesome God" (Ódhinn).

6. "The Father of Incantation (Magic)" (Ódhinn).

7. "The God of the Hanged" (Ódhinn).

8. The God of Hidden Things" or "The Hidden God" (Ódhinn).

9. Thórr is the slayer of the giant Hrungnir.

10. "The High One" (Ódhinn).

11. Freely adapted from the final stanzas of the "Hávamál."

12. Kvasir's blood is the poetic mead of inspiration, used here to invoke the vivifying magical power of that substance in the pigment.

13. Based on the ancient pre-Christian *vatni ausa* formula.

14. The possessive form of Æsir.

15. Sing the names and make the signs.

16. The kenning used in the original is *brynthings apaldr*, literally "apple tree of the court of byrnie."

17. *galdr* in original.

18. Literally translated this would read "Runes, whisper with correct advice."

Bibliography

Arntz, Helmut. *Handbuch der Runenkunde*. Halle/Saale; M. Niemeyer, 1944.

Blachetta, Walther. *Das Buch der deutschen Sinnzeichen*. Berlin-Lichterfelde; Widukind/Boss, 1941.

Ellis, Hilda R. *The Road to Hel*. Cambridge: Cambridge University Press, 1943.

Davidson, Hilda R. (Ellis). *Gods and Myths of Northem Europe*. Middlesex, UK: Penguin, 1964.

Dickins, Bruce. *Runic and Heroic Poems*. Cambridge: Cambridge University Press, 1915.

Dumezil. Georges. *Gods of the Ancient Northmen*. Edited by E. Haugen. Berkeley, CA: University of California Press, 1973.

Duwel, Klaus. *Runenkunde*. Sammlung Metzler 72, Stuttgart: J. B. Metzler. 1968.

Eliade, Mircea. *The Myth of the Eternal Return or Cosmos and History*. Translated by W. R. Trask. Bollingen Series 46, Princeton, NJ: Princeton University Press, 1971.

——————. *Shamanism: Archaic Techniques of Ecstasy*. Translated by W. R. Trask. Bollingen Series 46. Princeton, NJ: Princeton University Press, 1971.

Elliott, Ralph. *Runes, an Introduction*. Manchester: Manchester University Press, 1959.

Gorsleben, Rudolf John. *Die Hoch-Zeit der Menschheit*. Leipzig: Koeler & Amelang, 1930.

Grimm, Jacob. *Teutonic Mythology*. Translated by S. Stallybrass. 4 vols. New York: Dover, 1966.

Grönbech, Vilhelm. *The Culture of the Teutons*. London: Oxford Un iversity Press, 1931.

Hollander, Lee M., trans. *The Poetic Edda*. Austin, TX: University of Texas Press, 1962.

Krause, Wolfgang. *Was Man in Runen ritzte*. Halle/Salle: M. Niemeyer, 1935.

—————. *Die Runeninschriften im älteren Futhark*. Göttingen: Vandenhoeck & Ruprecht, 1966.

List, Guido von. *Die Bilderschrift der Ario-Germanen*. Leipzig: Guido-von-List-Gesellschaft, 1910.

—————. *Das Geheimnis der Runen*. Vienna: Guido-von-List-Gesellschaft, 1908.

Page, R.I. *An Introduction to English Runes*. London: Methuen, 1973.

Pálsson, Hermann, and Paul Edwards, trans., *Egil's Saga*. Middlesex, UK: Penguin, 1976.

Schneider, Karl. *Die Germanenischen Runenamen*. Meisenheim: Anton Hain, 1956.

Spiesberger, Karl. *Runenmagie*. Berlin: R. Schikowski, 1955.

—————. *Runenexerzitein fur Jedermann*. Frieburg: Bauer, 1976.

Sturluson, Snorri. *The Prose Edda*. Translated by A. G. Brodeur. New York: American Scandinavian Foundation, 1929.

Tacitus, Cornelius. *Germania*. Translated by H. Mattingly. Middlese, UK: Penguin, 1970.

Thorsson, Edred. *Runelore: A Handbook of Esoteric Runology*. York Beach: Weiser, 1987.

—————. *Runecaster's Handbook: The Well of Wyrd*. York Beach: Weiser, 1988.

—————. "The Medieval Icelandic 'Grammatical Treatises': What they Have to Teach the Runer." *Mainstays*. Smithville: The Rune-Gild, 2006, pp. 33-40.

—————. *Alu*. San Francisco: Weiser, 2012.

—————. *The Nine Doors of Midgard*. South Burlington: The Rune-Gild, 2016, 5th ed.

—————. *Rune-Writing: Our Original Way of Writing and The Key to Learning to Write Modern English in Anglo-Saxon Runes*. Bastrop: Runestar, 2020.

Turville-Petre, E.O.G. *Myth and Religion of the North*. New York: Holt Rinehart and Winston, 1964.

Vries, Jan de. *Altgermanische Religionsgeschichte*. 2 vols. Berlin: de Gruyter, 1956.

Also in Weiser Classics

The Book of Lies, by Aliester Crowley,
with an introduction by Richard Kaczynski

A Handbook of Yoruba Religious Concepts,
by Baba Ifa Karade

*The Herbal Alchemist's Kitchen: A Complete Guide
to Magickal Herbs and How to Use Them,*
by Karen Harrison, with a foreword by
Arin Murphy-Hiscock

*Psychic Self-Defense: The Definitive Manual for Protecting
Yourself Against Paranormal Attack,*
by Dion Fortune, with a foreword by Mary K. Greer

*Taking Up the Runes: A Complete Guide to Using Runes
in Spells, Rituals, Divination, and Magic,* by Diana L. Paxson

Yoga Sutras of Patanjali,
by Mukunda Stiles, with a foreword by Mark Whitwell

To Our Readers

Weiser Books, an imprint of Red Wheel/Weiser, publishes books across the entire spectrum of occult, esoteric, speculative, and New Age subjects. Our mission is to publish quality books that will make a difference in people's lives without advocating any one particular path or field of study. We value the integrity, originality, and depth of knowledge of our authors.

Our readers are our most important resource, and we appreciate your input, suggestions, and ideas about what you would like to see published.

Visit our website at *www.redwheelweiser.com* to learn about our upcoming books and free downloads and be sure to go to *www.redwheelweiser.com/newsletter* to sign up for newsletters and exclusive offers.

You can also contact us at *info@rwwbooks.com* or at

Red Wheel/Weiser, LLC
65 Parker Street, Suite 7
Newburyport, MA 01950